Canadian Living's™ best
BARBECUE

BY
Elizabeth Baird
AND
The Food Writers of Canadian Living Magazine
and The Canadian Living Test Kitchen

A MADISON PRESS BOOK
PRODUCED FOR
BALLANTINE BOOKS AND CANADIAN LIVING™

Ballantine Books
A Division of
Random House of
Canada Limited
1265 Aerowood Drive
Mississauga, Ontario
Canada
L4W 1B9

Canadian Living
Telemedia
Communications Inc.
50 Holly Street
Toronto, Ontario
Canada
M4S 3B3

Canadian Cataloguing in Publication Data

Barbecue

(Canadian Living's best)
ISBN 0-345-39797-5

1. Barbecue cookery.   I. Baird, Elizabeth.
II. Series.
TX840.B3B37 1994   641.7′6   C94-930275-9

Produced by
Madison Press Books
40 Madison Avenue
Toronto, Ontario
Canada
M5R 2S1

Printed in Canada

Contents

Introduction

Canadians are hopelessly hooked on barbecuing.

Maybe our long, dark winters make us appreciate the blessed warmth of outdoor summer living. Or maybe we just like the taste of grill-cooked food, kissed with smoke on the outside, juicy and moist inside.

For me it all started in the 1950s when my father built a stone barbecue in the backyard. To complete the scene, he put together a real picnic table, laid one of those new-fangled patios and invited relatives and friends over to enjoy the burgers he flipped himself, while wearing a joke apron and a floppy chef's hat.

Those old barbecues now look like relics beside the sleek, bubble-topped mini-ranges or handy hibachis parked on decks and patios countrywide. And "having a barbecue" has changed from being a special event to a daily activity. From burgers on Monday and grilled chicken on Tuesday to Friday-night pizza or a loin of pork for Sunday dinner — all can be cooked on the barbecue. And why not? Rain or shine, you flick the flame, and the lid keeps in the heat just like an oven.

The barbecuing season now stretches from the return of the robins well into chilly fall weekends and even, given a protected spot, until after the first snow. On a covered gas barbecue, Thanksgiving turkey, spring lamb and February T-bones are as possible as Canada Day burgers and August salmon. Sometimes even those who like the challenge of charcoal (and swear that food cooked over gas is not the same) will brave the elements for that elusive good-time, summer taste. And now gas and electric cooktop grills, countertop grill units, and single-burner grill attachments make that over-the-coals flavor possible anytime.

That's why all the recipes in *Canadian Living's Best Barbecue* have been carefully designed to help you get the most out of barbecuing (or grilling, as it's more correctly called), indoors or out, in warm or chilly weather — with or without the funny apron.

Elizabeth Baird

Beef at its Best

Nothing beats the appetite-quickening aroma of beef sizzling on a red-hot grill. Heat up the barbecue and sample a dozen new ways to enjoy this summer classic.

Provençal Beef Brochettes ▶

Serve these bountiful brochettes with rice or orzo drizzled with some of the Pesto Vinaigrette, crisp fresh greens and baguettes heated on the barbecue. The vinaigrette is also delicious tossed with potato salad.

1 lb	sirloin steak (1-1/2 inches/4 cm thick)	500 g
1	red onion	1
1	each sweet red and green pepper	1
1	small eggplant	1
12	mushroom caps	12
	Olive oil	
	Pesto Vinaigrette (recipe follows)	
	Salt and pepper	

● Cut beef into 1-1/2-inch (4 cm) cubes. Cut onion into similar-size chunks. Core, seed and cut red and green peppers into similar-size squares. Cut eggplant into 1-inch (2.5 cm) cubes.

● Alternately thread steak, onion, peppers, eggplant and mushrooms onto metal skewers; brush with oil. Let stand for 30 minutes.

● Place skewers on greased grill over high heat; cook for 2 minutes. Reserving half of the Pesto Vinaigrette, brush some of the remaining vinaigrette over brochettes.

● Cook, turning and basting occasionally with vinaigrette, for 10 to 12 minutes or until beef is medium-rare and vegetables are tender-crisp.

● Remove to platter and tent with foil; let stand for 5 minutes. Season with salt and pepper to taste. Serve with reserved vinaigrette. Makes 4 servings.

PESTO VINAIGRETTE

3	large cloves garlic, quartered	3
1 tsp	salt	5 mL
2 cups	packed fresh parsley	500 mL
1 cup	packed fresh basil (or 2 tbsp/25 mL dried)	250 mL
3 tbsp	red wine vinegar	50 mL
1 tsp	granulated sugar	5 mL
2/3 cup	olive oil	150 mL
	Pepper	

● In food processor, purée garlic and salt until pastelike. Add parsley and basil; process until fine paste. With motor running, add vinegar and sugar, then oil in thin, steady stream. Season with pepper to taste. Makes 1 cup (250 mL).

TIP: Whole pieces of meat (steaks, chops, roasts) you plan to grill or broil will always be more tender if you allow them to come to room temperature before cooking. However, monitor this carefully and do not allow meat to remain at summer temperatures for longer than 30 minutes.

T-Bone Steaks with Herb Garlic Butter

It's hard to beat a steak done on the grill and topped with a pat of garlicky butter. For accompaniments, split summer squash and slice red onions thickly; brush well with some of the steak marinade and grill alongside the T-bones. Round out the meal with barbecued potatoes (recipes, p. 76).

1/2 cup	olive oil	125 mL
1/4 cup	mixed minced fresh herbs (rosemary and basil or parsley)	50 mL
1/4 cup	dry vermouth or Marsala (optional)	50 mL
2 tbsp	minced shallots	25 mL
2 tsp	grated lemon rind	10 mL
2 tbsp	lemon juice	25 mL
4	T-bone steaks (3/4 inch/2 cm thick)	4
	Herb Garlic Butter (recipe follows)	
	Lemon wedges and herb sprigs	

● In food processor, blend oil, herbs, vermouth (if using), shallots, lemon rind and lemon juice. Brush over steaks; let stand for 30 minutes.

● Place steaks on greased grill over high heat; cook for 5 minutes on each side or until medium-rare, or to desired doneness.

● Remove steaks to plates; top each with pat of Herb Garlic Butter. Garnish with lemon and herb sprig. Makes 4 servings.

HERB GARLIC BUTTER

3 tbsp	butter, softened	50 mL
1 tbsp	each minced fresh basil, rosemary and parsley	15 mL
2 tsp	lemon juice	10 mL
2	cloves garlic, minced	2
Pinch	pepper	Pinch

● In bowl, combine butter, basil, rosemary, parsley, lemon juice, garlic and pepper. Cover and chill for up to 3 days. Makes 1/3 cup (75 mL).

Tender Marinated Steak ▶

Wine vinegar tenderizes leaner, tougher cuts of beef; fresh basil and garlic give them panache.

1 lb	inside round steak (1 inch/2.5 cm thick)	500 g
	WINE VINEGAR MARINADE	
1/3 cup	red wine vinegar	75 mL
3 tbsp	vegetable oil	50 mL
2 tbsp	chopped fresh basil	25 mL
1 tbsp	Dijon mustard	15 mL
2	cloves garlic, minced	2
1/4 tsp	pepper	1 mL

● WINE VINEGAR MARINADE: In shallow glass dish, combine vinegar, oil, basil, mustard, garlic and pepper; add steak, turning to coat.

● Cover and marinate in refrigerator for at least 12 hours or up to 24 hours, turning occasionally. Let stand at room temperature for 30 minutes.

● Reserving marinade, place steak on greased grill over medium-high heat; cook, brushing occasionally with marinade, for 7 to 8 minutes on each side for rare, 9 to 11 minutes for medium-rare, or 11 to 12 minutes for medium.

● Remove steak to cutting board; tent with foil and let stand for 5 minutes. Carve thinly across the grain on the diagonal. Makes 4 servings.

TIP: Inside round roasts, the most tender of the cheaper cuts of beef, are ideal for steaks. Buy a roast that weighs about 2 lb (1 kg), cut it in half horizontally and either double the recipe for a crowd, or freeze one steak for later use.

MORE MARINADES FOR STEAK

Each of these marinades makes enough for 1 lb (500 g) steak. For marinating and grilling times,
follow the recipe for Tender Marinated Steak (p. 8).

KOREAN MARINADE

1/4 cup	soy sauce	50 mL
2 tbsp	rice vinegar	25 mL
2 tbsp	vegetable oil	25 mL
1 tbsp	minced gingerroot	15 mL
1 tbsp	sesame oil	15 mL
2	cloves garlic, minced	2
1/4 tsp	pepper	1 mL

● In shallow glass dish, combine soy sauce, vinegar, vegetable oil, ginger, sesame oil, garlic and pepper. Makes 1/2 cup (125 mL).

BALSAMIC ROSEMARY MARINADE

1/4 cup	orange juice	50 mL
3 tbsp	vegetable oil	45 mL
2 tbsp	chopped fresh rosemary (or 1 tbsp/15 mL crumbled dried)	25 mL
2 tbsp	balsamic vinegar	25 mL
1 tbsp	Dijon mustard	15 mL
2	cloves garlic, minced	2
1/4 tsp	pepper	1 mL

● In shallow glass dish, combine orange juice, vegetable oil, rosemary, vinegar, mustard, garlic and pepper. Makes about 2/3 cup (150 mL).

GREEK MARINADE

2 tsp	grated lemon rind	10 mL
1/4 cup	lemon juice	50 mL
3 tbsp	vegetable oil	45 mL
2 tbsp	water	25 mL
2	cloves garlic, minced	2
2 tbsp	each chopped fresh oregano and mint (or 2 tsp/10 mL dried)	25 mL
1/4 tsp	pepper	1 mL

● In shallow glass dish, combine lemon rind and juice, oil, water, garlic, oregano, mint and pepper. Makes 1/2 cup (125 mL).

Lime and Mint-Glazed Flank Steak

Before marinating the steak in the Lime and Mint Glaze, set about 1/2 cup (125 mL) aside to pass around as a sauce. You can also use the glaze with lamb chops or butterflied leg of lamb.

1-3/4 lb	flank steak	875 g
	Lime and Mint Glaze (recipe follows)	
	Salt	
12	green onions, trimmed	12
	Lime wedges and mint sprigs	

● Place steak in dish; brush both sides with glaze. Cover and marinate in refrigerator for 4 hours, turning occasionally. Let stand at room temperature for 30 minutes.

● Brushing off and reserving marinade, place steak on greased grill over high heat; cook, brushing with marinade, for 7 to 8 minutes on each side or until medium-rare. Season with salt to taste. Remove to cutting board and tent with foil; let stand for 5 minutes.

● Meanwhile, brush onions with marinade; grill for 5 minutes or until golden brown.

● Carve steak thinly across the grain on the diagonal. Garnish platter with onions, lime and mint. Makes 4 to 6 servings.

	LIME AND MINT GLAZE	
2 tbsp	olive oil	25 mL
1	onion, minced	1
2	cloves garlic, minced	2
6	green onions, thinly sliced	6
1/4 cup	sherry or apple juice	50 mL
1 tbsp	grated lime rind	15 mL
2 tbsp	lime juice	25 mL
2 tbsp	grated gingerroot	25 mL
1 tbsp	granulated sugar	15 mL
1 tbsp	soy sauce	15 mL
1 cup	prepared mint sauce	250 mL

● In saucepan, heat oil over medium-high heat; cook minced onion, stirring often, for 3 to 5 minutes or until softened. Add garlic and green onions; cook for 3 to 4 minutes or until pale golden.

● Add sherry, lime rind and juice, ginger, sugar and soy sauce; cook for 2 minutes or until bubbly and slightly glossy.

● Stir in mint sauce and bring to simmer; cook over medium-low heat, stirring often, for 10 minutes or until reduced by one-quarter. Let stand for 2 hours. Makes 1-1/2 cups (375 mL).

TIP: Thicker steaks, such as flank steak, top round and sirloin, serve four to six. Instead of cutting the meat into portions, slice these steaks thinly across the grain on the diagonal. This makes the meat fork-tender.

Easy Alberta Sirloin Slab

Tender beef, well grilled, is a pleasure unto itself. But, to do it up right as they do in Alberta cattle country, serve it thickly sliced with Ranch-Country Barbecue Sauce (recipe, p. 73).

2	sirloin steaks, 2 inches (5 cm) thick (5 lb/2.2 kg total)	2
1 tbsp	coarsely ground pepper	15 mL

● Slash fat around steaks at 1-inch (2.5 cm) intervals; rub all over with pepper.

● Place steaks on greased grill over medium heat; cook, turning once with tongs, for about 15 minutes on each side for rare, 18 minutes for medium, or 20 minutes for well done.

● Remove steaks to cutting board and tent with foil; let stand for 5 minutes. Carve thinly across the grain on the diagonal. Makes 12 servings.

Grilled Steak Salad

1/3 cup	vegetable oil	75 mL
1/4 cup	red wine vinegar	50 mL
3/4 lb	flank steak	375 g
8 cups	torn mixed salad greens	2 L
Half	small Spanish, Vidalia or red onion, sliced	Half
1-1/4 cups	sliced strawberries (or 2 kiwifruit, sliced)	300 mL
	Salt and pepper	

● In shallow dish, whisk together 2 tbsp (25 mL) each of the oil and vinegar; add steak, turning to coat. Cover and marinate in refrigerator for at least 1 hour or up to 4 hours, turning occasionally. Let stand at room temperature for 30 minutes.

● Place steak on greased grill over medium-high heat; cook for 4 to 6 minutes on each side or until desired doneness. Remove to cutting board and tent with foil; let stand for 5 minutes. Carve steak thinly across the grain on the diagonal.

● In salad bowl, toss together greens, onion, steak and strawberries. Whisk together remaining oil and vinegar; toss with salad. Season with salt and pepper to taste. Makes 4 servings.

Grilled steak, sliced thinly and tossed with greens, is one answer to easy summer cooking. Halved cherry tomatoes and chopped sweet peppers can replace the fruit in the salad. Serve with warmed crusty French or Italian bread.

BEEF ON THE BARBECUE

CUTS OF STEAK
● The tenderest steaks come from the loin — T-bone, porterhouse, strip steaks and filets. If desired, add rubs or marinade for flavoring only.

● Cuts from the sirloin, located just behind the loin, are second in tenderness and suitable for grilling as a slab or for cutting into kabobs. Add rubs or marinade for flavoring only.

● Rib steaks follow in tenderness, but are so tasty that many people prefer them over loin or sirloin cuts.

● Medium to less tender cuts such as lean inside round and flank steaks need to be marinated, and are juicier if cooked just to medium-rare stage.

COOKING STEAKS AND ROASTS
● Let meat stand at room temperature for 30 minutes before grilling.

● Beef is leaner than ever and, except for pot roasts, is juicier if cooked no further than medium-rare.

● Cook steaks on uncovered grill and larger pieces of beef on covered grill (see Direct vs Indirect Heat, p. 46).

● Ideal thickness for steaks is at least 1 inch (2.5 cm). Ones up to 2 inches (5 cm) thick are even better as they allow the outside to brown and develop flavor while the inside remains pink and juicy.

● Trim off fat to about 1/4 inch (5 mm) and slash edges of steak at 1-inch (2.5 cm) intervals.

● To make sure everyone is served at the same time, place orders for "rare" on grill last.

● Turn steaks when bottom is well marked. Turn with tongs, never a fork, to avoid piercing meat and letting the juices run out.

● For a 1-inch (2.5 cm) thick steak over medium heat, allow 4 minutes on each side for rare, 5 minutes for medium and 6 minutes for well done.

● For less tender roasts such as short rib or blade, treat as a pot roast, wrapping in heavy foil with herbs, vegetables and a splash of wine or stock, and cooking on grill over medium to low heat or indirect heat (see p. 46) until tender and juicy. Unwrap and brown on all sides before carving.

● Boneless roasts, tied to form even-shaped piece, cook more evenly than bone-in roasts.

CHECKING FOR DONENESS
● To see if a steak is done, make a small slit in thickest part and check for desired color, or use the touch test: a rare steak is brown on the outside and feels soft and juicy through the center, medium is slightly firmer but still spongy and bouncy, while well-done is firm throughout.

● For roasts, insert meat thermometer in thickest part of meat, avoiding bone and fat: 140°F (60°C) for rare, 160°F (70°C) for medium, and 170°F (75°C) for well-done.

STANDING TIME
● Remove steaks and roasts from grill to cutting board and tent with foil. Let steaks stand for 5 minutes, roasts for up to 20 minutes, to allow the juices to spread evenly throughout the meat.

● Season with salt to taste before carving.

CARVING
● Always slice meat thinly across the grain on the diagonal to ensure that slices are fork-tender.

Fine Barbecued Rib Roast ▲

Roasts on the barbecue are even more succulent than roasts from the oven. Here, the best of all roasts, the rib roast (often called prime or standing rib), is cooked very simply to a rich glossy brown on the outside and juicy pink inside. If you like, brush with Ranch-Country Barbecue Sauce (recipe, p. 73) during the last 20 minutes of cooking.

1	standing rib roast of beef, boned and rolled with ribs (8 lb/3.5 kg)	1
1 tbsp	pepper	15 mL

● Let roast stand at room temperature for 1 hour; rub all over with pepper.

● Place roast on rack in barbecue roasting pan; place pan over medium heat. Close barbecue lid and cook for 3 to 3-1/2 hours or until meat thermometer registers 140°F (60°C) for rare, or 160°F (70°C) for medium. Remove roast to cutting board and tent with foil; let stand for 20 minutes.

● To serve, cut roast in half crosswise; carve rare slices from inside, and medium- to well-done slices from outside. Makes 12 servings.

TIP: When cooking roasts on the barbecue, it's a good idea to have a specially reserved shallow roasting pan so that good roasting pans are not blackened and ruined before their time. You'll still need to scrub this pan as clean as possible between grilling sessions, but you needn't worry about the blackened-on stuff you'll never get off. After a respectable time, the pan can be discarded.

Mushroom Barbecued Pot Roast

1-1/2 tsp	each dried thyme and dry mustard	7 mL
1/2 tsp	pepper	2 mL
1	chuck short rib or blade roast (4 lb/1.8 kg)	1
6 cups	sliced mushrooms (about 1 lb/500 g)	1.5 L
2 tbsp	beef stock or dry sherry	25 mL
1 tbsp	each vegetable oil and Worcestershire sauce	15 mL
	SAUCE	
	Beef stock	
1 tbsp	cornstarch	15 mL
2 tbsp	cold water	25 mL

● Combine thyme, mustard and pepper; rub all over roast.

● Sprinkle half of the mushrooms in middle of piece of heavy-duty foil large enough to wrap roast; place roast on top. Sprinkle with remaining mushrooms; drizzle with 2 tbsp (25 mL) stock and half of the oil. Loosely wrap foil over roast, sealing tightly; wrap with second piece of foil.

● Place roast on greased grill over medium heat; close lid and cook, turning often, for about 2 hours or until meat thermometer registers 170°F (75°C) for well done.

● Remove roast from foil, reserving mushrooms and juices in measuring cup for sauce. Place roast on grill; cook, turning once and brushing with remaining oil and Worcestershire sauce, for about 10 minutes longer or until browned. Remove roast to cutting board and tent with foil; let stand for 10 minutes before carving.

● SAUCE: Meanwhile, add enough stock to mushrooms and juices to make 2 cups (500 mL); pour into saucepan and bring to boil. Dissolve cornstarch in cold water; stir into pan and cook, stirring, for about 1 minute or until thickened and bubbly. Serve with roast. Makes 6 servings.

Less-than-tender cuts, wrapped in foil with herbs and mushrooms, roast to fork-only perfection on the barbecue.

Santa Fe Short Ribs

3 lb	lean beef short ribs, trimmed	1.5 kg
1	jar (7-1/2 oz/213 mL) hot salsa	1
1/2 cup	lime juice	125 mL
1 tbsp	vegetable oil	15 mL
2	cloves garlic, minced	2
1	small onion, finely chopped	1

● Place ribs in shallow glass dish. Stir together salsa, lime juice, oil, garlic and onion; pour over ribs. Cover and marinate in refrigerator for at least 2 hours or up to 4 hours, turning occasionally. Let stand at room temperature for 30 minutes.

● Place ribs and marinade on large piece of double thickness heavy-duty foil; loosely wrap over ribs, sealing tightly. Place on grill 6 inches (15 cm) from medium-high heat; close lid and cook, turning often, for about 1 hour or until ribs are tender. (To turn, place packet on plate and invert onto grill.)

● Unwrap ribs, reserving marinade in small bowl. Place ribs on greased grill over high heat; cook, turning and basting occasionally with marinade, for 10 to 15 minutes or until crisp and brown. Skim fat from any remaining marinade; pass marinade as sauce. Makes 4 servings.

Beef ribs, like pork ribs, need a tenderizing pre-cooking before a final crisping on the grill. And beef ribs deliver big taste for little money.

Devilled Beef Ribs

When you see "devilled" in a recipe title, you know you're in for something spicy! These bones, cut from standing rib roasts, are also meaty, succulent — and positively heavenly. Serve with ripe juicy tomatoes, grilled corn (see p. 81) and potato salad.

4 lb	meaty beef rib bones	1.8 kg
	Devil Sauce (recipe follows)	
	Salt and pepper	
1/4 cup	chopped fresh parsley	50 mL

● In large dish, arrange ribs in single layer. Remove about 1/2 cup (125 mL) of the Devil Sauce for dipping. Brush both sides of ribs with remaining Devil Sauce. Cover and marinate in refrigerator for 3 hours. Let stand at room temperature for 30 minutes.

● Reserving marinade, place ribs, curved side down, on greased grill over medium heat; cook, turning and brushing with marinade every 5 minutes, for 20 minutes. Season with salt and pepper to taste.

● Cook ribs for 3 to 5 minutes longer or until glazed and crusty. Remove to platter and tent with foil; let stand for 5 minutes. Sprinkle with parsley; cut into serving-size pieces and serve with remaining Devil Sauce. Makes 6 to 8 servings.

	DEVIL SAUCE	
1/4 cup	vegetable oil	50 mL
2 tbsp	butter	25 mL
1	large onion, minced	1
3	cloves garlic, minced	3
2 tbsp	packed brown sugar	25 mL
2 tbsp	lemon juice	25 mL
2 tsp	dried thyme	10 mL
1/4 tsp	cayenne pepper	1 mL
1/3 cup	each Dijon and grainy mustard	75 mL
1/4 cup	horseradish	50 mL
3/4 tsp	each salt and pepper	4 mL
1/4 tsp	(approx) hot pepper sauce	1 mL
1/4 cup	minced fresh parsley	50 mL

● In saucepan, heat oil and butter over medium-high heat; sauté onion for 3 to 5 minutes or until softened. Add garlic, sugar, lemon juice, thyme and cayenne; cook, stirring, for 4 to 5 minutes or until thickened. Let cool for 5 minutes.

● Whisk together Dijon and grainy mustards, horseradish, salt, pepper and hot pepper sauce; whisk into onion mixture. Add more hot pepper sauce, if desired; stir in parsley. Let cool. Makes 1-1/2 cups (375 mL).

Grilled Beef and Sweet Pepper Sandwiches

Italian or Portuguese rolls filled with smoky roasted peppers and juicy grilled beef are a grand way to use up leftovers.

1	sweet red pepper	1
2 tbsp	olive oil	25 mL
1 tbsp	Dijon mustard	15 mL
1-1/2 tsp	chopped fresh thyme	7 mL
1	clove garlic, minced	1
4	crusty rolls	4
4	lettuce leaves	4
1 cup	thinly sliced grilled beef	250 mL

● Place red pepper on grill over medium-high heat; cook, turning often, for about 20 minutes or until blistered and charred. Place in bowl; cover and let cool. Peel, seed and quarter lengthwise.

● Combine oil, mustard, thyme and garlic. Slice rolls in half lengthwise; spread cut sides with mustard mixture. Place rolls, cut sides down, on greased grill over medium heat; cook for 3 to 4 minutes or until golden. Sandwich lettuce, beef and red pepper in each roll. Makes 4 servings.

Barbecued Brisket of Beef Sandwich Feast

4 lb	fresh beef brisket	1.8 kg
	Smoky Barbecue Sauce (recipe follows)	
10	toasted hamburger buns or kaiser rolls	10

● Place brisket in large dish; pour in Smoky Barbecue Sauce. Cover and marinate in refrigerator for 24 hours, turning occasionally. Let stand at room temperature for 30 minutes.

● Place brisket on rack in barbecue roasting pan. Refrigerate 2 cups (500 mL) of the sauce for serving; use remaining sauce for basting.

● Place pan on grill over medium heat; pour in enough water to come 1/2 inch (1 cm) up sides of pan. Cover and cook, turning occasionally, basting generously with sauce and adding more water to maintain level, for 3 hours or until tender. Remove brisket to cutting board and tent with foil; let stand for 10 minutes.

● In saucepan, bring reserved sauce to boil; reduce heat and simmer for 2 minutes.

● Carve brisket thinly across the grain on the diagonal; pile into buns and drizzle with sauce. Pass any remaining sauce separately. Makes 8 to 10 servings.

SMOKY BARBECUE SAUCE

2 cups	bottled barbecue sauce	500 mL
1 cup	red pepper jelly	250 mL
1/4 cup	cider vinegar	50 mL
2 tbsp	Worcestershire sauce	25 mL
1 tbsp	liquid smoke	15 mL
1	bottle (375 mL) beer	1

● In saucepan, combine barbecue sauce, jelly, vinegar, Worcestershire sauce, liquid smoke and beer; bring to simmer over medium heat. Reduce heat to medium-low; simmer, uncovered, for 25 minutes or until glossy and thickened. Let cool to room temperature. Makes 4 cups (1 L).

Bring on the serviettes for this finger-stickin', finger-lickin' sandwich-style cookout. Halve and toast the buns, pile them up with thin slices of the brisket, add a generous spoonful of sauce and tuck in slices of sour dill pickle and red onion. Serve potato salad, a pot of baked beans and a tangy coleslaw alongside.

Curried Rice and Beef Salad

1-1/2 cups	parboiled rice	375 mL
1-1/2 cups	thinly sliced grilled beef	375 mL
1	small English cucumber, diced	1
1	large carrot, grated	1
1/2 cup	sliced radishes	125 mL
1/4 cup	sliced green onions	50 mL
1/4 cup	toasted slivered almonds	50 mL
	CURRY DRESSING	
1/3 cup	cider vinegar	75 mL
1/3 cup	vegetable oil	75 mL
2 tbsp	chopped fresh parsley	25 mL
4 tsp	chopped gingerroot	20 mL
1 tbsp	curry powder	15 mL
1 tbsp	liquid honey	15 mL
1-1/2 tsp	Dijon mustard	7 mL
1/2 tsp	each salt and pepper	2 mL

● In saucepan, bring 3 cups (750 mL) water to boil; add rice. Cover and reduce heat to low; simmer for about 20 minutes or until rice is tender and liquid absorbed. Let cool.

● CURRY DRESSING: Whisk together vinegar, oil, parsley, ginger, curry powder, honey, mustard, salt and pepper.

● In large salad bowl, combine rice, beef, cucumber, carrot, radishes and green onions; toss with dressing. Sprinkle with almonds. Makes 4 servings.

Fluffy rice, dressed with a curry vinaigrette, is tossed with leftover grilled beef and summer garden vegetables. One taste, and you'll know why rice salad is a rising star on the summer salad scene.

Pleasing Pork

From tangy kabobs and crowd-pleasing ribs to party-sized roasts, pork is always a delicious choice for summertime grills.

Micro-Grilled Korean Ribs

Korean ribs turn on the heat with hot pepper flakes (crushed chilies). Round out the "hands only" menu with grilled corn on the cob (see p. 81).

2 lb	pork spareribs	1 kg
1/3 cup	soy sauce	75 mL
1/4 cup	chopped green onion	50 mL
2 tbsp	sherry	25 mL
2 tsp	vegetable oil	10 mL
1 tsp	sesame oil	5 mL
1/4 tsp	hot pepper flakes	1 mL
1	clove garlic, minced	1
	Sesame seeds	

● Cut spareribs into serving-size pieces and arrange in shallow dish. Combine soy sauce, green onion, sherry, vegetable and sesame oils, hot pepper flakes and garlic; pour over ribs, turning to coat. Cover and marinate in refrigerator for at least 2 hours or up to 6 hours, turning often.

● Reserving marinade, arrange ribs in microwaveable dish; brush with 1/4 cup (50 mL) of the marinade.

● Cover and microwave at High for 5 minutes; microwave at Medium (50%) for 30 minutes, basting, turning and rearranging twice. Let stand for 5 minutes or until tender. If necessary, microwave at Medium (50%) for 5 to 10 minutes longer.

● Microwave reserved marinade at High for 1 minute or until boiling.

● Place ribs on greased grill over medium heat; cover and cook, turning and brushing with marinade, for 8 to 10 minutes or until browned. Sprinkle with sesame seeds. Makes 3 to 4 servings.

Sticky Red-Hot Ribs

These sweet-and-sour ribs are a summertime favorite. Chili sauce makes them sticky while zingy pepper sauce adds the fire. Highly recommendable accompaniments are grilled potatoes, Zucchinibobs (recipe, p. 80) and a heaping bowl of greens tossed with ranch-style dressing.

3 lb	pork spareribs	1.5 kg
1 cup	chili sauce	250 mL
3 tbsp	cider vinegar	50 mL
1 tbsp	dry mustard	15 mL
1 tbsp	packed brown sugar	15 mL
1 tbsp	Worcestershire sauce	15 mL
1 tsp	hot pepper sauce	5 mL
1/2 tsp	dried oregano	2 mL
Pinch	cayenne pepper	Pinch

● Cut spareribs into serving-size pieces and place in large pot; cover with water and bring to boil. Reduce heat, cover and simmer for 30 minutes or just until tender. Drain well and arrange in shallow dish.

● Meanwhile, in saucepan, combine chili sauce, vinegar, mustard, brown sugar, Worcestershire, hot pepper sauce, oregano and cayenne; bring to boil. Reduce heat and simmer for 2 minutes; let cool.

● Pour sauce over ribs, turning to coat well. Cover and marinate in refrigerator for at least 4 hours or up to 24 hours. Let stand at room temperature for 30 minutes.

● Reserving sauce, place ribs on greased grill over medium-high heat; cook, brushing with sauce occasionally and turning once, for 15 minutes or until browned. Makes 4 servings.

Oriental Black Bean Spareribs ▲

4 lb	pork spareribs	1.8 kg
1/2 cup	black bean sauce	125 mL
3 tbsp	rice vinegar	50 mL
2 tbsp	liquid honey	25 mL
2 tbsp	ketchup	25 mL
1 tbsp	sesame oil	15 mL
1 tbsp	chopped gingerroot	15 mL
2	cloves garlic, minced	2
Pinch	pepper	Pinch

● Cut spareribs into serving-size pieces and place in large pot; cover with water and bring to boil. Reduce heat, cover and simmer for about 40 minutes or until fork-tender. Drain well and arrange in shallow dish.

● Whisk together black bean sauce, vinegar, honey, ketchup, sesame oil, ginger, garlic and pepper; pour over ribs, turning to coat. Cover and marinate in refrigerator for at least 4 hours or up to 24 hours. Let stand at room temperature for 30 minutes.

● Reserving marinade, place ribs on greased grill over medium-high heat; cover and cook, turning and basting once with marinade, for about 10 minutes or until crisp and glazed. Makes 6 servings.

Black bean sauce has an assertive fermented flavor that grabs your tastebuds and never lets them go. What a delicious difference it makes to pork and seafood!

RIBS ON THE GRILL

● For spareribs, count on 3/4 lb (375 g) per serving for a feast, less for smaller appetites. Leave in strips or cut into 2- or 3-rib serving pieces, if desired. The meatiest ribs are back ribs, often called baby back ribs; less expensive side ribs, although not as meaty, still deliver on taste.

● Either precook ribs in water or in the microwave to tenderize them before brushing with sauce and crisping on the open grill — or cook them over low heat on covered barbecue, applying sauce during last 20 minutes to glaze and crisp ribs.

Barbecued Spareribs with Apple-Sage Glaze ◀

9 lb	pork spareribs	4 kg
4	cloves garlic, minced	4
2 tbsp	minced fresh sage	25 mL
1 tbsp	dry mustard	15 mL
1/2 tsp	salt	2 mL
1/4 tsp	pepper	1 mL
	GLAZE	
1	jar (500 mL) apple butter	1
1/2 cup	water	125 mL
1/4 cup	cider vinegar	50 mL
1 tbsp	each Dijon mustard and horseradish	15 mL
1 tbsp	packed brown sugar	15 mL
1/4 tsp	cayenne pepper	1 mL

● Place spareribs in large pot and cover with water; bring to boil. Reduce heat, cover and simmer for 45 to 60 minutes or until tender; drain well and let cool slightly.

● Combine garlic, sage, mustard, salt and pepper; rub over ribs. Arrange in large dish; cover and marinate in refrigerator for at least 30 minutes or up to 24 hours. Let stand at room temperature for 30 minutes.

● GLAZE: In small saucepan, stir together apple butter, water, vinegar, mustard, horseradish, brown sugar and cayenne; bring to boil. Reduce heat and simmer, stirring often, for 15 minutes; let cool. Cover and refrigerate until grilling time.

● Place glaze on side of grill to heat. Place ribs on greased grill over low heat; cook, turning every 10 to 15 minutes and brushing with glaze during last 15 minutes, for 30 to 45 minutes or until crisp.

● Cut ribs into serving-size pieces. Pass remaining glaze as sauce. Makes 12 servings.

Apple butter is a staple in farmers' markets and most supermarkets throughout Southwestern Ontario. In other parts of the country, look for this tangy apple spread at your local deli. Serve ribs with potato salad and fresh garden vegetables.

Peking Ribs

3 lb	pork spareribs	1.5 kg
8	whole peppercorns	8
1	clove garlic, sliced	1
1 tsp	salt	5 mL
2 tbsp	cornstarch	25 mL
1/4 cup	soy sauce	50 mL
1 cup	cold strong tea	250 mL
2 tbsp	red wine vinegar	25 mL
1 tbsp	minced gingerroot	15 mL
2 tsp	liquid honey	10 mL
1 tbsp	packed brown sugar	15 mL

● Cut ribs into 2- or 3-rib portions and place in large pot; cover with water. Add peppercorns, garlic and salt; bring to boil. Reduce heat, cover and simmer for 50 minutes or until tender. Drain well and place in plastic bag set in bowl.

● In saucepan, dissolve cornstarch in soy sauce; whisk in tea, vinegar, ginger and honey. Pour half of the mixture over ribs; close bag and marinate at room temperature for 30 minutes or in refrigerator for 2 hours. Remove from refrigerator 30 minutes before cooking.

● Stir brown sugar into remaining tea mixture. Cook over medium-high heat, stirring constantly, for about 5 minutes or until thickened. Remove from heat.

● Discarding marinade, place ribs on greased grill over medium heat; cook for 6 minutes on each side or until browned. Brush with thickened tea mixture; cook for 2 minutes. Turn and brush again; cook for 2 minutes or until glazed. Makes 4 servings.

As glossy as Peking duck, these ribs have a surprise ingredient — cold tea! — which mellows the Oriental flavors of soy sauce and ginger.

Hoisin Orange Pork Chops

Transform everyday pork chops into company fare by adding a few easy-to-find tastes of Southeast Asia.

4	pork loin chops (about 3/4 inch/2 cm thick)	4
2 tbsp	hoisin sauce	25 mL
2 tbsp	vinegar	25 mL
2 tbsp	orange juice concentrate	25 mL
2 tbsp	soy sauce	25 mL
1 tbsp	peanut butter	15 mL
1 tsp	sesame oil	5 mL
2	cloves garlic, minced	2
1 tbsp	minced gingerroot	15 mL

● Trim excess fat from chops; arrange in shallow dish.

● Combine hoisin sauce, vinegar, orange juice concentrate, soy sauce, peanut butter, sesame oil, garlic and ginger; pour over chops, turning to coat. Cover and marinate in refrigerator for at least 1 hour or up to 24 hours. Let stand at room temperature for 30 minutes.

● Reserving marinade, place chops on greased grill over medium heat; cook, basting occasionally with marinade, for about 5 minutes on each side or just until no longer pink inside. Makes 4 servings.

Beer-Marinated Barbecued Pork Chops ▶

This marinade capitalizes on the slight bitterness that beer drinkers cherish. Any beer, with or without alcohol, can be used. Serve with Embered Onions (recipe, p. 81) and sweet potatoes.

4	pork loin chops (about 3/4 inch/2 cm thick)	4
	BEER MARINADE	
1/4 cup	beer	50 mL
1/4 cup	rice vinegar	50 mL
2 tbsp	canola oil	25 mL
1 tbsp	molasses	15 mL
1 tsp	salt	5 mL
1/2 tsp	pepper	2 mL
1/4 tsp	cinnamon	1 mL

● Trim excess fat from chops; arrange in shallow dish.

● BEER MARINADE: In jar with tight-fitting lid, shake together beer, vinegar, oil, molasses, salt, pepper and cinnamon; pour over chops, turning to coat. Cover and marinate in refrigerator for at least 4 hours or up to 24 hours. Let stand at room temperature for 30 minutes.

● Reserving marinade, place chops on greased grill over medium heat; cook, turning and brushing with marinade once, for about 10 minutes or just until no longer pink inside. Makes 4 servings.

MORE MARINADES FOR PORK CHOPS

Each marinade makes enough for 4 pork chops, 1 lb (500 g) in total. Any beer can be used. For marinating and grilling times, follow the recipe for Beer-Marinated Barbecued Pork Chops (above).

OSAKA-STYLE MARINADE

2 tbsp	canola oil	25 mL
2 tbsp	rice vinegar	25 mL
2 tbsp	thick teriyaki sauce	25 mL
1 tbsp	grated gingerroot	15 mL
2 tsp	sesame oil	10 mL
2	cloves garlic, minced	2

● In glass jar with tight-fitting lid, shake together canola oil, vinegar, teriyaki sauce, ginger, sesame oil and garlic. Makes 1/3 cup (75 mL).

HONEY-MUSTARD MARINADE

1/4 cup	beer	50 mL
2 tbsp	canola oil	25 mL
2 tbsp	liquid honey	25 mL
2 tbsp	each Dijon and grainy mustards	25 mL
1 tsp	coarse black pepper	5 mL

● In glass jar with tight-fitting lid, shake together beer, canola oil, honey, Dijon and grainy mustards and pepper. Makes 2/3 cup (150 mL).

Apple Thyme Pork Chops

Whether it's apple or thick slices of pineapple and melon, grilled fruit makes a juicy accompaniment for pork, chicken and fish.

4	pork loin chops (about 3/4 inch/2 cm thick)	4
1/4 cup	apple juice	50 mL
1/4 cup	lemon juice	50 mL
1 tbsp	cider vinegar	15 mL
1 tbsp	vegetable oil	15 mL
1/2 tsp	dried thyme	2 mL
2	apples, peeled and quartered	2
2 tbsp	liquid honey	25 mL

● Trim excess fat from chops; arrange in shallow dish.

● Stir together apple juice, lemon juice, vinegar, oil and thyme; pour over chops, turning to coat. Cover and marinate in refrigerator for at least 2 hours or up to 4 hours. Let stand at room temperature for 30 minutes.

● Reserving marinade in small saucepan, place chops on greased grill over medium heat; cook, turning once, for 10 minutes or until still slightly pink inside.

● Meanwhile, boil marinade for 3 minutes. Dip apples into marinade and place on grill.

● Stir honey into marinade; brush generously over chops and apples. Cook, turning apples often, for about 5 minutes longer or just until pork is no longer pink inside and apples are tender. Makes 4 servings.

Real Barbecued Pork

Competitors at New Westminster, B.C.'s annual barbecue championship are experts at authentic barbecuing — slow cooking with smoke, not quick death by fire. Here's one of the winning recipes for superlative, succulent pork.

1/4 cup	coarse salt	50 mL
6 lb	pork shoulder (bone in)	2.7 kg
1 tbsp	hickory liquid smoke	15 mL
3 cups	large spinach leaves	750 mL

● Spread salt in shallow baking dish. Brush pork with liquid smoke. Roll in salt until completely covered.

● Wrap pork in 2 layers of spinach; tie at 3-inch (8 cm) intervals with kitchen string. Place on large piece of heavy-duty foil; loosely wrap over pork, sealing tightly.

● Place, fat side down, on grill over low heat; cook for about 3 hours or until meat thermometer registers 160°F (70°C). Remove to cutting board and let stand for 20 minutes. Unwrap and remove spinach before carving. Makes 10 servings.

PORK ON THE BARBECUE

● Choose pork chops or steaks for quick suppers. Marinate or apply rubs more for flavor than tenderness because meat cut from the loin is very tender.

● For maximum moistness, choose chops at least 3/4 inch (2 cm) thick. Trim fat to 1/4-inch (5 mm) thickness and slash at 1-inch (2.5 cm) intervals.

● Grill larger pieces of pork on the barbecue with lid closed to reduce possible flare-ups, using indirect heat (see p. 46) and a drip pan placed directly under roast.

● For maximum tenderness and juiciness, cook pork over medium heat only until it has just lost its pinkness or until meat thermometer registers 160°F (70°C).

● Check doneness of roasts and large cuts by using meat thermometer inserted into thickest part, avoiding bone and fat. After cooking, tent with foil and let stand for 10 to 15 minutes before carving.

Beer-Glazed Picnic Shoulder ▼

2/3 cup	packed brown sugar	150 mL
1/4 tsp	whole cloves	1 mL
3 lb	boneless cooked smoked picnic shoulder	1.5 kg
1/2 cup	beer or apple juice	125 mL
1 tbsp	all-purpose flour	15 mL
1 tbsp	dry mustard	15 mL
2 tbsp	vinegar	25 mL

● In small bowl, stir together brown sugar and cloves. Place picnic shoulder on large piece of heavy-duty foil; set in barbecue roasting pan. Press half of the sugar mixture on top; drizzle with beer. Loosely wrap foil over meat, sealing tightly.

VEGETABLES IN PACKETS

Foil packets of potatoes, carrots, onions or other favorite vegetables cooked right on the barbecue are a quick and easy way to round out a summertime grill. For a delicious selection, see p. 77.

● Set pan on grill over medium heat; close lid and cook, turning wrapped meat once, for 1 hour.

● Stir flour and mustard into remaining sugar mixture; blend in vinegar.

● Remove meat from foil and pan; place on greased grill. Cook, brushing often with sugar mixture and turning occasionally, for 15 minutes or until well glazed.

● Remove to cutting board and tent with foil; let stand for 10 minutes before slicing. Makes 8 servings.

Smoked picnic shoulder is just as tasty as ham, but less expensive. Chop leftovers to toss into pasta, rice or potato salads.

Party-Size Barbecued Pork Roast

In the world of real barbecue — slow cooking of large pieces of meat to develop a rich and smoky deep-down flavor — there is controversy. Is it better to rub the meat with a flavorful dry mixture, or slather it with a wet sauce? This prizewinning recipe from one of British Columbia's annual barbecue competitions uses both — to perfection!

6 lb	boneless pork loin (double loin)	2.7 kg
	Cranberry Relish (recipe follows)	
	SPICE RUB	
1 tbsp	salt	15 mL
1 tbsp	granulated sugar	15 mL
1-1/2 tsp	pepper	7 mL
1 tsp	paprika	5 mL
1/2 tsp	grated lemon rind	2 mL
1/2 tsp	dry mustard	2 mL

● SPICE RUB: Combine salt, sugar, pepper, paprika, lemon rind and mustard; rub all over pork. Wrap pork with plastic wrap and refrigerate for at least 12 hours or up to 24 hours. Remove plastic wrap; let stand at room temperature for 30 minutes.

● Place pork on greased grill over low heat; cover and cook for 1-1/2 hours. Cook, brushing often with some of the Cranberry Relish, for 1 hour longer or until meat thermometer registers 160°F (70°C).

● Remove to cutting board and tent with foil; let stand for 20 minutes before carving. Pass remaining Cranberry Relish separately. Makes 16 to 20 servings.

	CRANBERRY RELISH	
1-1/2 cups	cranberry jelly	375 mL
1/2 cup	packed brown sugar	125 mL
2 tbsp	grated orange rind	25 mL
2 tsp	pepper	10 mL

● In saucepan, bring jelly, sugar, orange rind and pepper to simmer; cook over low heat, stirring, for about 3 minutes or until smooth. Makes about 1-1/2 cups (375 mL).

Grilled Teriyaki Pork Tenderloin

Lean, tender and quick, tenderloin makes up for its higher cost by being all meat and no waste. Like other cuts of pork, the tenderloin's sweetness is a perfect match with Japanese teriyaki.

2	pork tenderloins (each 3/4 lb/375 g)	2
	TERIYAKI MARINADE	
1/3 cup	soy sauce	75 mL
1/4 cup	vegetable oil	50 mL
1/4 cup	sherry	50 mL
1/4 cup	ketchup	50 mL
2 tsp	white wine vinegar	10 mL
2	green onions, chopped	2
1	clove garlic, minced	1
1 tbsp	minced gingerroot	15 mL
Pinch	each salt and pepper	Pinch

● Tuck ends under and tie each tenderloin with string. Place in shallow glass dish.

● TERIYAKI MARINADE: Whisk together soy sauce, oil, sherry, ketchup, vinegar, onions, garlic, ginger, salt and pepper; pour over meat and turn to coat. Cover and marinate at room temperature for 30 minutes or in refrigerator for at least 2 hours or up to 4 hours, turning occasionally. Remove from refrigerator 30 minutes before cooking.

● Measure out 1/4 cup (50 mL) of the marinade for brushing; pour remainder into small saucepan.

● Place pork on greased grill over medium heat; cook, turning halfway through and brushing occasionally with marinade, for about 25 minutes or just until no longer pink inside.

● Meanwhile, bring reserved marinade to boil; reduce heat and simmer for 2 minutes. Serve with pork. Makes 6 servings.

Curry Lime Kabobs ▲

1	pork tenderloin (3/4 lb/375 g)	1
1/2 tsp	grated lime rind	2 mL
2 tbsp	lime juice	25 mL
2 tbsp	chopped fresh coriander or parsley	25 mL
1 tbsp	packed brown sugar	15 mL
1 tbsp	vegetable oil	15 mL
2 tsp	curry powder	10 mL
1/4 tsp	salt	1 mL
Pinch	pepper	Pinch
1	large sweet yellow pepper	1

● Cut pork into 1-1/2-inch (4 cm) cubes; place in bowl.

● Whisk together lime rind and juice, coriander, sugar, oil, curry powder, salt and pepper; add to bowl and toss to coat. Cover and marinate at room temperature for 30 minutes or in refrigerator for up to 2 hours. Remove from refrigerator 30 minutes before cooking.

● Cut yellow pepper into chunks about same size as pork. Reserving any marinade, alternately thread pork and yellow pepper onto each of 4 soaked wooden skewers.

● Place on greased grill over medium heat; cook, turning occasionally and basting with marinade, for 15 minutes or just until pork is no longer pink inside. Makes 2 servings.

The hint of curry complements both the pork and the fruit. Sliced star fruit (carambola) is the garnish of choice, but pineapple or papaya can also add a touch of the tropics.

Tangy Pork Kabobs ▼

Skewers of succulent pork team up deliciously with summer's best — sweet, juicy corn on the cob and field-ripened tomatoes.

1 lb	lean boneless pork	500 g
1	sweet green pepper	1
1/4 cup	apple juice	50 mL
2 tbsp	lemon juice	25 mL
1 tbsp	olive or vegetable oil	15 mL
1 tbsp	soy sauce	15 mL
2 tsp	packed brown sugar	10 mL
1 tsp	dry mustard	5 mL

● Cut pork into 3/4-inch (2 cm) cubes. Core, seed and cut green pepper into 3/4-inch (2 cm) chunks. Alternately thread pork and green pepper loosely onto soaked wooden skewers.

● In small bowl, whisk together apple and lemon juices, oil, soy sauce, sugar and mustard; brush some of the mixture all over kabobs.

● Place on greased grill over medium-high heat; cook, basting often and turning occasionally, for 15 to 18 minutes or just until pork is no longer pink inside. Makes 4 servings.

Souvlaki

1-1/2 lb	boneless pork shoulder, trimmed	750 g
1	clove garlic, minced	1
1/4 tsp	each salt and pepper	1 mL
1/4 cup	olive oil	50 mL
1/4 cup	dry red wine or lemon juice	50 mL
1 tbsp	dried oregano	15 mL

● Cut pork into 1-1/2-inch (4 cm) cubes; place in bowl. Toss with garlic, salt and pepper. Cover and refrigerate for at least 1 hour or up to 24 hours. Let stand at room temperature for 30 minutes.

● In bowl, whisk together oil, wine and oregano. Thread 2 or 3 cubes of meat onto each skewer; place on greased grill over medium heat; cook, turning once and basting frequently with oil mixture, for 20 to 25 minutes or just until no longer pink inside. Makes 4 servings.

It's hard to believe that anything this simple can be this good! Serve these skewers of tender pork as an appetizer or main course, wrapping the cubes of pork in a pita bread or torpedo bun and drizzling with Yogurt Mint Sauce (recipe, p. 60).

Fajitas with Peppers and Apples

2 cups	thinly sliced grilled pork	500 mL
2	sweet peppers, julienned	2
1	red onion, thinly sliced	1
1	tart apple (unpeeled), sliced	1
1/2 tsp	hot pepper flakes	2 mL
1/4 tsp	salt	1 mL
	Chopped fresh coriander and slivered green onion top	
6	flour tortillas, warmed	6
1/3 cup	each salsa and sour cream	75 mL

● In large heavy greased skillet over medium-high heat, stir-fry pork, sweet peppers, onion, apple, hot pepper flakes and salt for 7 minutes or until vegetables are tender-crisp. Transfer to platter; garnish with coriander and green onion.

● Spoon mixture into tortillas, dollop with salsa and sour cream and roll up. Makes 6 servings.

Here's a surefire way of getting everyone in the household to enjoy grilled pork the second time round.

Thai-Style Pork Salad

1/4 cup	thick teriyaki sauce	50 mL
2 tbsp	each canola oil and water	25 mL
1 tsp	grated lime rind	5 mL
4 tsp	lime juice	20 mL
1/2 tsp	hot pepper sauce	2 mL
2 cups	thinly sliced grilled pork	500 mL
4 cups	shredded mixed salad greens	1 L
2 cups	cooked vermicelli or spaghettini	500 mL
1/4 cup	each chopped fresh mint and coriander	50 mL
	Chopped red onion	

● Whisk together teriyaki sauce, oil, water, lime rind and juice and hot pepper sauce. Pour half over pork in glass bowl; cover and marinate in refrigerator for 1 hour.

● In large bowl, toss together salad greens, vermicelli, mint, coriander and remaining marinade; transfer to platter. Top with pork; garnish with onion. Makes 4 servings.

Why barbecue for every meal when you can barbecue one night and use the grill-enhanced meat for a second meal? Here, leftover pork from any grilled roast or chops makes an encore in a Thai-inspired salad.

Honey Mustard Sausages

2 lb	farmer's sausage	1 kg
1/4 cup	prepared mustard	50 mL
2 tbsp	liquid honey	25 mL
1/2 tsp	dried basil	2 mL

Take a crusty roll, cradle a mustard-and-basil-coated sausage in it and you have a delightful summer meal — zesty, easy and appealing. For kid-style meals, choose milder sausages.

● In large skillet, cover sausage with water; bring to boil. Reduce heat to medium-low and simmer, covered, for 12 minutes. Drain well; cut into thirds.

● Meanwhile, in bowl, stir together mustard, honey and basil.

● Place sausage pieces on greased grill over medium-high heat; cook, turning often, for 5 minutes. Cook, brushing with mustard mixture, for 5 minutes longer. Makes 6 servings.

TIP: To microwave instead of simmering the sausage, place on microwaveable rack; prick, cover with waxed paper and microwave at High for 2 minutes. Turn, prick and cover with waxed paper; microwave at High for 2 to 4 minutes longer or until no longer pink inside. Let stand for 3 minutes.

Grilled Sausage on a Bun ▶

Any mild sausage will taste just as good split and topped with a fresh-tasting tomato salsa.

4	white German sausages (weisswurt)	4
2 tbsp	olive oil	25 mL
4	crusty rolls, halved lengthwise	4
1	clove garlic, halved	1
	TOMATO SALSA	
2	tomatoes, seeded and diced	2
1	green onion, chopped	1
2 tbsp	chopped fresh basil or parsley	25 mL
2 tsp	olive oil	10 mL
1-1/2 tsp	white wine vinegar	7 mL
	Salt and pepper	

● TOMATO SALSA: In bowl, combine tomatoes, onion, basil, oil and vinegar; season with salt and pepper to taste; set aside.

● Prick sausages all over with fork; brush with 1 tsp (5 mL) of the oil. Place on greased grill over medium-high heat; cook, turning occasionally, for 20 to 25 minutes or until cooked through.

● Meanwhile, brush remaining oil over cut sides of rolls; place on grill and cook for 1 to 2 minutes or until toasted. Rub with cut side of garlic. Halve sausages lengthwise; place in rolls. Drain tomato salsa and divide among rolls. Makes 4 servings.

SAUSAGES ON THE GRILL

Search out the best sausages you can find to barbecue. Peppery farmer's sausage is great on the grill, and so are Italian, Portuguese, Greek, Macedonian, German and Eastern European sausages. Make sure you buy fresh, not dried, sausages to grill. Freshly smoked sausages are also an easy barbecue item — and there's no need to pre-simmer. Just grill and slice thinly into appetizer-size tidbits.

Sizzling Lamb

Lamb was a late arrival on the Canadian barbecue scene, but now it's definitely here to stay — with tender kabobs and chops, special-occasion racks and glorious butterflied leg of lamb.

Lamb Kabobs

A hint of coriander gives this summertime lamb an authentic Middle Eastern flavor. Serve with a fresh cucumber salad, hummus and pita bread.

1 lb	lean lamb	500 g
3 tbsp	vegetable oil	50 mL
1 tbsp	sesame oil	15 mL
1 tsp	ground coriander	5 mL
1/2 tsp	caraway seeds, crushed	2 mL
1/4 tsp	pepper	1 mL
1	bay leaf	1
4	firm ripe tomatoes	4
4	small onions	4
2 tbsp	chopped fresh parsley	25 mL
	Salt	

● Cut lamb into 1-inch (2.5 cm) cubes; place in bowl. Combine vegetable and sesame oils, coriander, caraway seeds, pepper and bay leaf; add to lamb, stirring to coat well.

● Cover and marinate in refrigerator for at least 1 hour or up to 4 hours, stirring occasionally. Let stand at room temperature for 30 minutes. Discard bay leaf.

● Cut tomatoes in half; cut onions in half through root end. Reserving marinade, thread meat alternately with tomatoes and onions onto greased metal skewers.

● Place on greased grill over medium-high heat; cook, turning and basting with marinade, for 12 to 15 minutes or until lamb is medium-rare. Sprinkle with parsley, and salt to taste. Makes 4 servings.

TIP: To give the lamb added flavor, soak fresh rosemary sprigs in water, then place them on the coals while cooking the kabobs.

Herbed Lamb Chops

The punchy assertiveness of rosemary suits lamb to a "T." For a dazzling presentation, thread chops onto skewers along with chunks of summer-fresh vegetables.

1/4 cup	olive oil	50 mL
2 tbsp	chopped fresh thyme	25 mL
1 tbsp	chopped fresh rosemary	15 mL
2	large cloves garlic, minced	2
1 tbsp	red wine vinegar	15 mL
8	lamb loin chops, 1 inch (2.5 cm) thick	8
	Salt and pepper	

● In shallow dish, combine oil, thyme, rosemary, garlic and vinegar; add lamb chops, turning to coat well. Cover and marinate in refrigerator for 8 hours or up to 24 hours, turning occasionally. Let stand at room temperature for 30 minutes.

● Place lamb chops on greased grill over medium-high heat; cook for 5 to 7 minutes on each side for medium-rare or until desired doneness. Season with salt and pepper to taste. Makes 4 servings.

LAMB ON THE GRILL

● Since lamb sold in Canada comes from young animals, it is tender and should be cooked until medium-rare so that its pink juiciness can be enjoyed.

● For open-barbecue grilling, choose the tenderest cuts — butterflied leg of lamb, boneless loins, racks and chops. Marinate or apply rubs for flavoring only.

● Less tender shoulder cuts should be marinated in the refrigerator for up to 1 day and then cooked, covered, using indirect heat (see p. 46).

● Let lamb stand at room temperature for 30 minutes before grilling.

● Choose chops that are at least 3/4 inch (2 cm) thick. Trim off fat to 1/4-inch (5 mm) thickness and slash fat at 1-inch (2.5 cm) intervals.

● Transfer grilled meat to cutting board and tent with foil. Let chops stand for 5 minutes, larger cuts for up to 15 minutes, to allow the juices to spread evenly throughout the meat.

Lamb Chops à la Madame Benoit ▼

Jehane Benoit, for many years the doyenne of Canadian cooking, is the creator of this simple lemon and basil marinade. It makes culinary magic with loin or rib chops.

1/4 cup	lemon juice	50 mL
2 tbsp	vegetable oil	25 mL
1 tbsp	chopped fresh basil	15 mL
3/4 tsp	pepper	4 mL
1	clove garlic, crushed	1
3/4 tsp	Dijon mustard	4 mL
8	lamb loin chops, 1 inch (2.5 cm) thick	8
	Salt	

● In shallow dish, combine lemon juice, oil, basil, pepper, garlic and mustard; add lamb chops, turning to coat well. Cover and marinate at room temperature for 30 minutes or in refrigerator for 4 hours, turning occasionally. Remove from refrigerator 30 minutes before cooking.

● Reserving marinade, place chops on greased grill over medium-high heat; cook, basting twice with marinade, for 5 to 7 minutes on each side for medium-rare or until desired doneness. Sprinkle with salt to taste. Makes 4 servings.

Lamb Chops with Red Pepper Pesto ▲

8	lamb loin chops, about 3/4 inch (2 cm) thick	8
	Oil, salt and pepper	
	Red Pepper Pesto (recipe follows)	

2 tbsp	freshly grated Parmesan cheese	25 mL
2	cloves garlic, minced	2
	Salt and pepper	

● Brush lamb chops lightly with oil. Place on greased grill over medium-high heat; cook for 5 to 7 minutes on each side for medium-rare or until desired doneness. Season with salt and pepper to taste. Serve with Red Pepper Pesto. Makes 4 servings.

RED PEPPER PESTO		
2	sweet red peppers	2
1/2 cup	fresh basil leaves	125 mL
3 tbsp	olive oil	50 mL

● Place peppers on greased grill over medium-high heat; cook, turning frequently, for about 20 minutes or until charred all over. Let cool enough to handle; peel, core and seed.

● In food processor, purée peppers until smooth. Add basil, oil and cheese; purée until well blended. Stir in garlic, and salt and pepper to taste. Makes 1 cup (250 mL).

A purée of roasted sweet red peppers dresses up grilled lamb — and is equally delicious with barbecued fish, beef or chicken. The pesto lasts up to 2 days in the refrigerator but may need a splash more olive oil to thin it before serving.

Orange-Glazed Leg of Lamb ▲

You can rely on barbecued boneless lamb for great party food. Add a cold rice salad to the menu, plus crusty bread and cold asparagus spears lightly napped with vinaigrette.

1	butterflied leg of lamb (3 lb/1.5 kg)	1
2 tbsp	olive oil	25 mL
1 tbsp	(approx) coarsely grated orange rind	15 mL
1/4 cup	orange juice	50 mL
2 tsp	chopped fresh rosemary	10 mL
3 tbsp	orange marmalade, heated and strained	45 mL
	Salt and pepper	

● Trim fat from lamb. In large shallow dish, combine oil, orange rind, orange juice and rosemary; add lamb and turn to coat well. Cover and marinate in refrigerator for at least 8 hours or up to 24 hours, turning occasionally. Let stand at room temperature for 30 minutes.

● Discarding marinade, place lamb on greased grill over medium-high heat; cook, turning four times and basting with marmalade on both sides during last 10 minutes, for 25 to 30 minutes for rare or until meat thermometer registers 140°F (60°C), or 35 to 40 minutes for medium-rare (150°F/65°C).

● Remove to cutting board and tent loosely with foil; let stand for 10 minutes before carving. Serve garnished with more orange rind. Makes 8 to 10 servings.

TIP: To ensure that butterflied leg of lamb cooks evenly, insert four metal skewers — two horizontally and two vertically — through the various muscles that make up the leg, forming the meat into a compact shape and even thickness. The skewers will also help when turning the lamb.

Grilled Racks of Lamb with Thyme

4	racks of lamb, chinebone removed (3 lb/1.5 kg total)	4
1/4 cup	red wine	50 mL
2 tbsp	olive oil	25 mL
2 tbsp	chopped fresh thyme (or 4 tsp/20 mL dried)	25 mL
4 tsp	anchovy paste	20 mL
2 tsp	red wine vinegar	10 mL
1/2 tsp	pepper	2 mL
	Salt	

● Remove almost all fat from lamb racks, leaving 1/8 inch (3 mm) layer. Place in shallow glass dish.

● In small dish, mix wine with oil, thyme, anchovy paste, vinegar and pepper. Brush over lamb. Cover and marinate at room temperature for 30 minutes or in refrigerator for up to 8 hours. Remove from refrigerator 30 minutes before cooking.

● Reserving any marinade, place lamb, fat side down, on greased grill over medium-high heat; cook, turning often and brushing with marinade, for about 25 minutes or until fat is golden-crisp and meat thermometer registers 140°F (60°C) for rare or until desired doneness.

● Remove to cutting board and tent with foil; let stand for 10 minutes. Sprinkle with salt to taste; carve into 2-rib portions. Makes 8 servings.

For two, a rack of lamb is a wonderful indulgence. For guests, just increase the number of racks. Serve with Gremolada Tomatoes (recipe, p. 78) and grilled potato skewers.

TIP: Always ask butcher to remove chinebone (backbone) from racks of lamb. Otherwise, it is impossible to cut between the ribs.

Balsamic Butterflied Lamb

1	butterflied leg of lamb (3 lb/1.5 kg)	1
1/4 cup	Dijon mustard	50 mL
2 tbsp	balsamic vinegar	25 mL
1 tbsp	olive oil	15 mL
2	cloves garlic, minced	2
1 tsp	dried thyme	5 mL
Pinch	each salt and pepper	Pinch

● Trim fat from lamb. In large shallow dish, combine mustard, vinegar, oil, garlic and thyme. Add lamb and turn to coat well. Cover and let stand at room temperature for 30 minutes.

● Place lamb on greased grill over medium-high heat; cook, turning four times, for 25 to 30 minutes for rare or until meat thermometer registers 140°F (60°C), or 35 to 40 minutes for medium-rare (150°F /65°C). Remove to cutting board and tent loosely with foil; let stand for 10 minutes before carving. Makes 8 to 10 servings.

A butterflied leg of lamb says easy but elegant summer entertaining. Add new potatoes and fresh yellow and green beans to the menu — and relax!

Lamb Shoulder with Thyme and Garlic

1	boned lamb shoulder (2 lb/1kg)	1
2 tbsp	chopped fresh thyme	25 mL
2 tbsp	minced garlic	25 mL
2 tbsp	olive oil	25 mL
	Salt and pepper	

● Flatten and trim lamb; place in large shallow dish. Combine thyme, garlic and oil; spread all over lamb. Cover and marinate in refrigerator for at least 8 hours or up to 24 hours. Let stand at room temperature for 30 minutes.

● Place lamb on greased grill over medium-high heat; cover and cook, turning once, for 12 to 15 minutes on each side or until meat thermometer registers 140°F (60°C) for rare or 160°F (70°C) for medium. Remove to cutting board and tent with foil; let stand for 10 minutes before carving. Season with salt and pepper to taste. Makes 4 servings.

Thyme and garlic combine to accent the flavor of lamb. Let this simple marinade work its magic on lamb chops, too.

The Choicest Chicken

Chicken is delicious cooked almost any way — but on the grill, the combination of smoky, juicy and crispy flavors is irresistible.

Chicken and Veggie Packets

Chicken and seasonal vegetables team up for one-pack servings. This recipe can be halved for two, or doubled and tripled when unexpected guests drop in for supper.

4	boneless skinless chicken breasts	4
2 tbsp	cornstarch	25 mL
2	small zucchini, sliced	2
4	small tomatoes, cut into wedges	4
2	onions, cut into wedges	2
1/4 cup	red wine vinegar	50 mL
1/4 cup	olive oil	50 mL
2 tbsp	each chopped fresh basil and oregano	25 mL
1	clove garlic, minced	1
Pinch	each granulated sugar, salt and pepper	Pinch

● Cut four 12-inch (30 cm) squares of heavy-duty foil; brush lightly with oil. Place chicken breast in center of each; dust with cornstarch. Top evenly with zucchini, tomatoes and onions.

● Whisk together vinegar, oil, basil, oregano and garlic; drizzle over vegetables. Sprinkle with sugar, salt and pepper. Loosely wrap foil over chicken, using double fold to seal tightly. *(Chicken can be prepared to this point and refrigerated for up to 8 hours.)*

● Place packets on grill over medium-high heat; cook, turning once, for 20 minutes or until chicken is no longer pink inside. Makes 4 servings.

Prosciutto-Wrapped Chicken Breasts ▶

Prosciutto ham is not smoked, yet it adds a big burst of flavor to barbecued chicken — and keeps it moist and juicy on the grill.

4	boneless skinless chicken breasts	4
4 tsp	Dijon mustard	20 mL
1-1/2 tsp	chopped fresh sage	7 mL
8	slices prosciutto or ham	8
	Fresh sage leaves	

● Using small sharp knife and beginning at thick side, cut two-thirds of the way through each breast to form pocket. Brush inside of pockets with half of the mustard; sprinkle with chopped sage.

● Close pockets; brush remaining mustard over top of breasts. Wrap 2 slices prosciutto around each breast; tuck ends underneath.

● Place chicken on greased grill over medium-high heat; cook, turning once, for 12 minutes or until no longer pink inside. Garnish with sage leaves. Makes 4 servings.

MARINADES FOR CHICKEN

Each marinade makes enough for 2 lb (1 kg) chicken. For marinating and grilling times,
follow the recipe for Herb and Buttermilk Barbecued Chicken (p. 39).

LEMON PEPPER MARINADE

3/4 cup	buttermilk	175 mL
1 tbsp	finely grated lemon rind	15 mL
1/4 cup	lemon juice	50 mL
2 tbsp	vegetable oil	25 mL
2 tbsp	Dijon mustard	25 mL
1 tbsp	coarsely cracked black pepper	15 mL
2	cloves garlic, minced	2
2 tsp	dried oregano	10 mL
1/4 tsp	each salt and cayenne pepper	1 mL

● In large bowl, whisk together buttermilk, lemon rind and juice, oil, mustard, pepper, garlic, oregano, salt and cayenne. Makes 1-1/3 cups (325 mL).

LIME CUMIN MARINADE

3/4 cup	buttermilk	175 mL
	Grated rind and juice of 3 limes	
2 tbsp	vegetable oil	25 mL
2	cloves garlic, minced	2
1 tbsp	dried mint	15 mL
1 tbsp	ground cumin	15 mL
1/4 tsp	each salt and pepper	1 mL

● In large bowl, whisk together buttermilk, lime rind and juice, oil, garlic, mint, cumin, salt and pepper. Makes 1-1/3 cups (325 mL).

THAI MARINADE

3/4 cup	buttermilk	175 mL
1/3 cup	canned coconut cream	75 mL
2 tbsp	vegetable oil	25 mL
2 tbsp	fish sauce	25 mL
2 tsp	dried basil	10 mL
1 tsp	hot pepper flakes	5 mL
1 tsp	grated gingerroot	5 mL
2	cloves garlic, minced	2
1/2 cup	chopped fresh coriander	125 mL
1/4 tsp	each salt and pepper	1 mL

● In large bowl, whisk together buttermilk, coconut cream, oil, fish sauce, basil, hot pepper flakes,, ginger, garlic, coriander, salt and pepper. Marinate for 4 hours only. Makes 1-1/2 cups (375 mL).

Herb and Buttermilk Barbecued Chicken ◄

2 lb	chicken parts, skinned	1 kg
	BUTTERMILK MARINADE	
3/4 cup	buttermilk	175 mL
2 tbsp	vegetable oil	25 mL
2 tbsp	Dijon mustard	25 mL
2	cloves garlic, minced	2
2 tsp	each dried oregano, basil, thyme and rosemary	10 mL
1/4 tsp	each salt and pepper	1 mL

● BUTTERMILK MARINADE: In large bowl, whisk together buttermilk, oil, mustard, garlic, oregano, basil, thyme, rosemary, salt and pepper.

● Add chicken, turning to coat. Cover and marinate in refrigerator for at least 4 hours or up to 24 hours, turning occasionally. Let stand at room temperature for 30 minutes.

● Reserving marinade, place chicken on greased grill over medium heat; cook, turning occasionally and brushing with marinade, for 30 to 40 minutes or until juices run clear when chicken is pierced. Makes 4 servings.

Buttermilk is low in fat yet it has a rich and creamy consistency that's perfect for coating and marinating. It also keeps this chicken moist and succulent on the grill — no mean feat when the chicken is skinned.

Rosemary Mustard Chicken Breasts

4	boneless skinless chicken breasts	4
5	cloves garlic, minced	5
2 tbsp	minced fresh rosemary	25 mL
2 tbsp	grainy mustard	25 mL
2 tbsp	lemon juice	25 mL
2 tbsp	olive oil	25 mL
	Salt and pepper	

● In shallow glass dish, arrange chicken in single layer. Combine garlic, rosemary, mustard, lemon juice and oil; pour over chicken, turning to coat. Cover and marinate at room temperature for 30 minutes.

● Place chicken on greased grill over medium-high heat; cook, turning once, for 12 to 15 minutes or until no longer pink inside. Season with salt and pepper to taste. Makes 4 servings.

This flavorful dish is special enough for entertaining yet easy enough for quick weekday suppers. For two, divide ingredients in half, using only 2 cloves of garlic.

Five-Spice Grilled Chicken Breasts

4	chicken breasts	4
3	green onions, minced	3
2	large cloves garlic, minced	2
2 tbsp	packed brown sugar	25 mL
2 tbsp	each fish sauce and soy sauce	25 mL
2 tbsp	dry sherry	25 mL
1/2 tsp	five-spice powder	2 mL
1/2 tsp	salt	2 mL
1/4 tsp	pepper	1 mL
1/4 tsp	chili paste	1 mL
2 tbsp	chopped fresh coriander	25 mL

● In shallow glass dish, arrange chicken in single layer. Whisk together onions, garlic, sugar, fish sauce, soy sauce, sherry, five-spice powder, salt, pepper and chili paste. Pour over chicken, turning to coat. Cover and marinate in refrigerator for 2 hours or up to 4 hours. Let stand at room temperature for 30 minutes.

● Place chicken, skin side down, on greased grill over medium-high heat; cook, turning once, for 20 minutes. Brush with any remaining marinade; cook, turning once, for 5 to 10 minutes longer or until no longer pink inside. Garnish with coriander. Makes 4 servings.

Aromatic Oriental five-spice powder — made up of equal parts cinnamon, cloves, fennel seed, star anise and Szechuan peppercorns — can now be found in many supermarkets. Serve this deliciously spiced chicken with rice or rice noodle salad and steamed pea pods.

Jerk Chicken on the Grill

At its most authentic, the mixture of hot and spicy seasoning for jerk chicken is only for the most adventurous palates. This tamer version is ideal for casual entertaining. Round out the menu with creamy coleslaw and rice.

4	boneless skinless chicken breasts	4
2	green onions, coarsely chopped	2
2 tbsp	orange juice	25 mL
4 tsp	soy sauce	20 mL
1 tsp	granulated sugar	5 mL
1 tsp	each allspice and pepper	5 mL
1 tsp	vinegar	5 mL
1/2 tsp	dried thyme	2 mL
1/4 tsp	each nutmeg and curry powder	1 mL
Pinch	hot pepper flakes	Pinch
2	cloves garlic, minced	2

● In shallow glass dish, arrange chicken in single layer.

● In food processor, combine green onions, orange juice, soy sauce, sugar, allspice, pepper, vinegar, thyme, nutmeg, curry powder and hot pepper flakes. Pulse several times to purée; stir in garlic.

● Pour over chicken, turning to coat. Cover and marinate in refrigerator for at least 2 hours or up to 4 hours. Let stand at room temperature for 30 minutes.

● Place chicken on greased grill over medium-high heat; cook, turning once, for 8 to 12 minutes or until no longer pink inside. Makes 4 servings.

Skewers of Chicken and Zucchini

Add to the eye appeal of these summertime kabobs by using both green and gold zucchini.

4	boneless skinless chicken breasts	4
2	zucchini	2
1	red onion	1
1/4 cup	olive oil	50 mL
2 tbsp	coarsely grated lemon rind	25 mL
1/4 cup	lemon juice	50 mL
3	green onions, minced	3
5	cloves garlic, minced	5
1/2 tsp	salt	2 mL
1/2 tsp	pepper	2 mL
Dash	hot pepper sauce	Dash

● Cut chicken into 1-1/2-inch (4 cm) pieces. Cut zucchini into 1/2-inch (1 cm) thick slices. Cut red onion into eighths. Arrange in single layer in shallow glass dish.

● In small bowl, combine olive oil, lemon rind and juice, green onions, garlic, salt, pepper and hot pepper sauce; pour over chicken mixture. Marinate at room temperature for 30 minutes or in refrigerator for up to 4 hours. Remove from refrigerator 30 minutes before cooking.

● Reserving marinade, thread slice of zucchini, piece of chicken, zucchini slice, onion wedge, another zucchini slice, chicken piece and final zucchini slice onto skewer. Repeat with remaining chicken and vegetables.

● Place skewers on greased grill over medium-high heat; cook, brushing with marinade and turning occasionally, for about 20 minutes or until chicken is no longer pink inside and vegetables are tender. Makes 4 servings.

TIP: Be sure to soak wooden skewers for 30 minutes before using to prevent scorching.

Hoisin Orange Chicken Legs ▲

4	chicken legs	4
1/4 cup	hoisin sauce	50 mL
1 tsp	grated orange rind	5 mL
1/4 cup	orange juice	50 mL
2	cloves garlic, minced	2
1 tbsp	minced gingerroot	15 mL
1 tbsp	vegetable oil	15 mL
1 tbsp	Seville orange marmalade	15 mL

● Place chicken in shallow glass dish. Stir together hoisin sauce, orange rind and juice, garlic, ginger and oil; pour over chicken, turning to coat. Cover and marinate in refrigerator for at least 3 hours or up to 8 hours, turning occasionally. Let stand at room temperature for 30 minutes.

● Reserving marinade in small saucepan, place chicken on greased grill over medium-high heat; cook, turning often, for 15 minutes.

● Meanwhile, bring marinade to boil; stir in marmalade and keep warm on grill. Brush generously over chicken; cook, basting and turning often, for 10 to 15 minutes or until juices run clear when chicken is pierced. Makes 4 servings.

An easy glaze zests up chicken. Round out the Oriental flavors with rice or bean salad and steamed sugarsnap peas.

Micro-Grilled Moroccan Chicken ◄

4	chicken legs	4
	Salt and pepper	
	MARINADE	
1	small onion, chopped	1
1/3 cup	olive oil	75 mL
1/4 cup	fresh mint leaves	50 mL
2 tsp	grated lemon rind	10 mL
1/4 cup	lemon juice	50 mL
2 tsp	ground cumin	10 mL
2 tsp	paprika	10 mL
1 tsp	granulated sugar	5 mL
1	clove garlic, minced	1
1/2 tsp	pepper	2 mL
1/4 tsp	ground ginger	1 mL

● Pierce chicken in several places; arrange in 11- x 17-inch (2 L) microwaveable dish.

● MARINADE: In food processor or blender, combine onion, oil, mint, lemon rind and juice, cumin, paprika, sugar, garlic, pepper and ginger; purée until smooth. Spread over chicken; cover and marinate in refrigerator for 2 hours, turning once. Let stand at room temperature for 30 minutes.

● Arrange chicken with thickest parts to outside of dish. Cover with vented plastic wrap and microwave at High, turning pieces and basting twice, for 8 to 10 minutes or until juices run clear when chicken is pierced.

● Reserving marinade, place chicken on greased grill over medium heat; cook, basting occasionally with marinade, for 5 minutes on each side or until golden. Season with salt and pepper to taste. Makes 4 servings.

The microwave teams up with the barbecue to produce crispy-on-the-outside, juicy-on-the-inside cumin-scented chicken in no time at all. Serve with almond-studded couscous and cucumbers.

Cajun Chicken Livers

1 lb	chicken livers	500 g
2 tbsp	vegetable oil	25 mL
2	cloves garlic, minced	2
2 tsp	pepper	10 mL
1 tsp	each salt and paprika	5 mL
1 tsp	dry mustard	5 mL
1/2 tsp	cayenne pepper	2 mL
1/4 tsp	each dried thyme and oregano	1 mL

● Trim livers; pat dry and place in bowl. Combine oil and garlic; toss with livers.

● Combine pepper, salt, paprika, mustard, cayenne, thyme and oregano; sprinkle over livers and mix well.

● Place livers on greased grill over medium-high heat; cook, turning once, for 6 to 8 minutes or until browned yet still pink inside. Makes 4 servings.

Even if you think you don't like liver, you'll want to give these barbecued morsels a try — they're crisp and spicy on the outside, and tender and juicy inside. Liver never tasted this good!

CHICKEN ON THE BARBECUE

● Always remove visible fat from whole chickens and parts before cooking.

● Let chicken stand at room temperature for 30 minutes before placing on heated grill.

● Apply honey-, sugar- or tomato-based sauces or marinades only during the last 10 to 15 minutes of cooking to prevent scorching.

● Cook poultry through. Breasts and wings should no longer be pink inside. For legs and thighs, juices should run clear when meat is pierced.

● Whole chickens and halves are done when meat thermometer inserted in thickest part of thigh registers 185°F (85°C).

● Transfer grilled chicken to cutting board and tent with foil. Let chicken pieces stand for 5 minutes, whole birds or halves for 10 minutes, to allow juices to spread evenly throughout the meat.

Maple-Glazed Thighs

Cheaper than breasts, moist and tender chicken thighs glaze up golden brown and sticky-good on the grill.

1/4 cup	maple syrup	50 mL
2 tbsp	vegetable oil	25 mL
2 tsp	soy sauce	10 mL
1-1/2 tsp	lemon juice	7 mL
8	chicken thighs	8
	Sesame seeds (optional)	

● In small bowl, combine maple syrup, oil, soy sauce and lemon juice; set aside.

● Place chicken, meaty side down, on greased grill over medium-high heat; cover and cook, turning once, for 10 minutes.

● Turn chicken and baste with syrup mixture; cook, turning and basting again, for 10 minutes or until juices run clear when chicken is pierced. Sprinkle with sesame seeds (if using). Makes 4 servings.

Lemon Rosemary Chicken ▼

Utterly simple — and unbelievably good! These words sum up summertime cooking and these chicken legs.

6	chicken legs	6
1/3 cup	olive oil	75 mL
1/4 cup	lemon juice	50 mL
2 tbsp	chopped fresh rosemary	25 mL
2	cloves garlic, minced	2
2 tbsp	Dijon mustard	25 mL
	Salt and pepper	

● Place chicken in large shallow dish. Whisk together oil, lemon juice, rosemary and garlic; pour over chicken, turning to coat. Cover and marinate at room temperature for 30 minutes or in refrigerator for up to 2 hours. Remove from refrigerator 30 minutes before cooking.

● Reserving marinade, place chicken, meaty side up, on greased grill over medium heat; cover and cook, turning once, for 25 to 30 minutes or until golden brown.

● Stir mustard into reserved marinade; brush over chicken and cook, turning and brushing with marinade, for 12 to 15 minutes or until juices run clear when chicken is pierced. Season with salt and pepper to taste. Makes 6 servings.

A TASTE OF ITALY ON THE GRILL

Head out to the backyard for an Italian-inspired alfresco feast — and let your barbecue do the rest! Start with colorful Yellow Pepper and Tomato Bruschetta (p. 84). Then, while the Lemon Rosemary Chicken (above) is grilling to perfection, add sausages and your favorite vegetables on skewers. Prick sausages and microwave for 5 minutes (or poach in covered skillet for 12 minutes), then grill until evenly browned. *Buon appetito*!

(clockwise from top) Yellow Pepper and Tomato Bruschetta, Lemon Rosemary Chicken, vegetable skewers, grilled sausages.

Teriyaki Chicken and Vegetable Slaw

36	snow peas, trimmed	36
4	green onions	4
1	large carrot	1
1/3 cup	coarsely chopped cashews	75 mL
3 cups	large strips grilled skinless chicken	750 mL
2 cups	thinly shredded Napa or Chinese cabbage	500 mL
	DRESSING	
2 tbsp	rice vinegar	25 mL
2 tbsp	vegetable oil	25 mL
4 tsp	teriyaki sauce	20 mL
1 tsp	packed brown sugar	5 mL
2	cloves garlic, minced	2
1 tsp	sesame oil	5 mL
1/4 tsp	hot pepper sauce	1 mL

● DRESSING: In salad bowl, whisk together vinegar, vegetable oil, teriyaki sauce, sugar, garlic, sesame oil and hot pepper sauce; set aside.

● In pot of boiling water, blanch snow peas for 30 seconds or until tender-crisp; drain, refresh under cold water and pat dry.

● Thinly slice onions on the diagonal. With vegetable peeler, pare carrot into thin strips.

● In ungreased skillet, toast cashews over medium heat, stirring, for 3 minutes or until lightly browned.

● Add snow peas, onions, carrot, chicken and cabbage to dressing in bowl; toss to combine. Garnish with cashews. Makes 4 servings.

Grill enough chicken for an encore performance in this Pacific Rim salad.

LIGHTENED-UP CHICKEN

● The fat in chicken can be reduced by discarding the skin. With skin, a whole leg rings up about 13 g fat and a single breast about 8 g. Taking the skin off subtracts about 5 g from each, for a final total of about 8 g for a whole leg and 3 g for a single breast.

● One chicken breast or leg, about (3 oz/90 g), provides about 28 g of high-quality protein, more than half a woman's daily need.

Grilled Chicken and Tomato Salad

3 cups	bite-size pieces crusty bread	750 mL
3 cups	bite-size pieces grilled skinless chicken	750 mL
3	tomatoes, cubed	3
1/3 cup	black olives, halved	75 mL
Quarter	white onion, sliced	Quarter
4 cups	torn mixed salad greens	1 L
	DRESSING	
2 tbsp	red wine vinegar	25 mL
1 tsp	Dijon mustard	5 mL
1/4 tsp	each salt and pepper	1 mL
1/3 cup	olive oil	75 mL
1/4 cup	each chopped fresh basil and parsley	50 mL

● DRESSING: In large bowl, whisk together vinegar, mustard, salt and pepper; gradually whisk in oil. Stir in basil and parsley; set aside.

● Spread bread on baking sheet; bake in 375°F (190°C) oven for about 15 minutes or until golden. Let cool.

● Add bread, chicken, tomatoes, olives and onion to dressing; toss well. Arrange lettuce on plates; top with salad. Makes 4 servings.

Crusty Italian bread, oil-cured black olives and garden-ripened tomatoes make this main-course salad a summer star.

Summer Grilled Chicken

*Glossed and accented with
spices, these chicken legs are
featured on our cover along
with Beer-Marinated
Barbecued Pork Chops
(p. 20), Roasted Garlic and
Gremolada Tomatoes (p. 78).*

4	chicken legs	4
3 tbsp	vegetable oil	50 mL
1 tbsp	red wine vinegar	15 mL
1	clove garlic, minced	1
1 tsp	dry mustard	5 mL
1/2 tsp	paprika	2 mL
1/4 tsp	each dried thyme and salt	1 mL
Pinch	pepper	Pinch

● Place chicken in shallow glass dish. Whisk together oil, vinegar, garlic, mustard, paprika, thyme, salt and pepper; pour over chicken, turning to coat. Cover and marinate in refrigerator for at least 8 hours or up to 24 hours. Let stand at room temperature for 30 minutes.

● Reserving marinade, place chicken, meaty side up, on greased grill over medium heat; cook for 15 minutes. Turn and cook, basting occasionally with marinade, for 15 to 25 minutes longer or until juices run clear when chicken is pierced. Makes 4 servings.

Thai Barbecued Chicken

*Using indirect heat to grill a
whole chicken (see sidebar
below) allows it to cook
through without charring the
outside. The Thai ingredients
— fish sauce, lime and fresh
coriander — are delicious
with chicken parts, too.*

1	chicken (4 lb/1.8 kg)	1
2 tbsp	fish sauce	25 mL
2 tbsp	lime juice	25 mL
2 tbsp	hoisin sauce	25 mL
1 tbsp	vegetable oil	15 mL
2 tsp	packed brown sugar	10 mL
1/2 tsp	sesame oil	2 mL
1/4 tsp	each ground coriander and ginger	1 mL
	Coriander sprigs	

● Remove neck and giblets from chicken. Rinse and pat chicken dry inside and out. In small bowl, whisk together fish sauce, lime juice, hoisin sauce, vegetable oil, sugar, sesame oil, coriander and ginger; brush 2 tbsp (25 mL) over cavity. Tie legs together with string; tuck wings under back.

● Heat one burner of barbecue to medium-high. Place chicken, breast side down, on greased grill over unlit side of barbecue. Brush with some of the fish sauce mixture; cover and cook for 45 minutes.

● Turn chicken over; baste with fish sauce mixture. Cover and cook, basting every 20 minutes, for 1-3/4 to 2-1/4 hours or until meat thermometer inserted in thickest part of thigh registers 185°F (85°C).

● Remove to cutting board and tent with foil; let stand for 10 minutes before carving. Garnish with coriander. Makes 6 servings.

WHICH HEAT TO USE?

DIRECT HEAT
Direct heat cooks food directly over heat source, and cooks it quickly with more browning. The barbecue may be open or covered. Use for steaks, chops and burgers.

INDIRECT HEAT
With the indirect method, food is not cooked directly over heat source. The barbecue is covered and acts like an oven, preventing flare-ups. Use for roasts, whole poultry and thick food.

● **For gas barbecue with two or more burners:** On one side of barbecue, place food on grill over drip pan; turn off burner under drip pan, leaving other burner(s) on. Cook as directed.

● **For charcoal barbecue with cover:** Move hot coals to sides of barbecue; put drip pan between coals. Place food on grill over drip pan. Cook as directed.

Barbecued Turkey ▼

12 lb	turkey	5.4 kg
	GLAZE	
1/3 cup	white wine vinegar	75 mL
1/3 cup	vegetable oil	75 mL
2 tbsp	chopped fresh rosemary, sage or thyme (or 2 tsp/10 mL dried)	25 mL
1 tsp	Dijon mustard	5 mL

● Remove neck and giblets from turkey. Rinse and pat turkey dry inside and out. Secure neck skin to back, tie wings to body, tuck in or tie legs together securely with string.

● GLAZE: Whisk together vinegar, oil, rosemary and mustard; set aside.

● Place turkey, breast side up, on greased grill over indirect medium heat (see sidebar, p. 46). Close lid and cook, brushing several times with glaze, for about 3 hours or until meat thermometer inserted in center of thigh next to body registers 185°F (85°C).

● Remove to cutting board and tent with foil; let stand for 10 minutes before carving. Makes 6 to 8 servings.

Celebrate Thanksgiving with an end-of-season barbecue. A 12-pound (5.4 kg) turkey is ideal; anything much larger will take too long to cook and will dry out. Do not stuff turkey; bake your favorite stuffing separately. Garnish grilled turkey with some of the stuffing, if you like, and serve the rest alongside.

Catch of the Day

From curried cod and glorious whole salmon to lime-splashed lobster and nineties-style calamari, it's no wonder fish and seafood are such hot news on the barbecuing scene.

Prizewinning Barbecued Salmon

Slow-barbecuing a whole fillet of salmon is one glorious — and relaxing! — way to entertain. Buy a fillet as evenly thick as possible to prevent the thinner tail end from drying out before the rest of the fillet is cooked through.

5	large cloves garlic, chopped	5
1/4 tsp	salt	1 mL
2 tbsp	finely chopped fresh parsley	25 mL
2 tbsp	olive oil	25 mL
1 tbsp	minced sun-dried tomatoes	15 mL
1	salmon fillet (unskinned), 2 lb (1 kg)	1

● In bowl, mash garlic with salt; combine with parsley, oil and tomatoes. Cover and refrigerate for at least 8 hours or up to 12 hours.

● Place salmon, skin side down, on greased grill over low heat. Brush half of the garlic mixture over top; cook for 15 minutes.

● Brush salmon with remaining garlic mixture; increase heat to medium and cook for about 10 minutes or until fish flakes easily when tested with fork. Makes 6 servings.

Grilled Salmon Fillets ▶

Choose a thick, skin-on fillet and let the salmon soak up the flavorful marinade before grilling.

1	salmon fillet (unskinned), 1 lb (500 g)	1
	LIME MARINADE	
1/4 cup	olive oil	50 mL
1 tsp	grated lime rind	5 mL
1/4 cup	lime juice	50 mL
4 tsp	Worcestershire sauce	20 mL
1-1/2 tsp	ground cumin	7 mL
2	cloves garlic, minced	2
1/4 tsp	each salt and pepper	1 mL

● On cutting board, slice salmon fillet into 4 pieces. If necessary, remove any bones with tweezers. Measure thickest portion of fillet to determine cooking time.

● LIME MARINADE: In shallow glass dish, whisk together olive oil, lime rind and juice, Worcestershire sauce, cumin, garlic, salt and pepper; add fillets. Using tongs, turn to coat evenly. Cover and marinate in refrigerator for up to 30 minutes, turning occasionally.

● Reserving marinade, place fillets, skin side down, on greased grill over medium-high heat; cook, basting frequently with marinade and turning once halfway through, for 10 minutes per inch (2.5 cm) of thickness or until fish flakes easily when tested with fork and flesh is opaque. Makes 4 servings.

TIP: Be sure to marinate fish only as long as specified; otherwise, it will "cook" in the acids of the marinade and become dry during grilling.

Cod with Lemon-Dill Mayo

Tangy lemon mayonnaise coats cod fillets to keep them moist on the grill, then serves as a refreshing sauce.

1 lb	cod fillets	500 g
1/2 cup	light mayonnaise	125 mL
2 tbsp	plain yogurt	25 mL
1 tsp	grated lemon rind	5 mL
2 tbsp	lemon juice	25 mL
1 tsp	dried dillweed	5 mL
1/4 tsp	pepper	1 mL

● Pat fish dry. Stir together mayonnaise, yogurt, lemon rind and juice, dillweed and pepper; brush about one-third all over fish. Place in greased grilling basket; close basket.

● Place on grill over high heat; cook, turning once, for 5 to 8 minutes or until fish flakes easily when tested with fork. Serve with remaining mayonnaise mixture. Makes 4 servings.

TIP: If you don't have a hinged basket — the perfect gadget to hold delicate flaky fish — use two lifters, one under the fish and one over, to support the fish while turning.

Oriental Fish Kabobs with Green Onions

Serve these quick-cooking kabobs with rice or a rice salad. For extra flavor and color, add generous amounts of chopped sweet red pepper and fresh peas to the rice.

1 lb	monkfish fillets, 1 inch (2.5 cm) thick	500 g
2 tbsp	soy sauce	25 mL
2 tbsp	dry sherry	25 mL
1 tbsp	oyster sauce	15 mL
1-1/2 tsp	minced gingerroot	7 mL
1 tsp	lemon juice	5 mL
1 tsp	sesame oil	5 mL
1/4 tsp	pepper	1 mL
8	green onions	8

● Cut fish into 1-inch (2.5 cm) chunks; place in bowl.

● Combine soy sauce, sherry, oyster sauce, ginger, lemon juice, sesame oil and pepper; pour over fish and stir gently to coat. Cover and marinate at room temperature for 30 minutes or in refrigerator for up to 1 hour.

● Cut white and pale green parts of onions into 2-inch (5 cm) lengths.

● Reserving marinade, alternately thread fish and onions onto skewers. Place on greased grill over medium-high heat; cook, turning once and brushing with marinade, for about 6 minutes or until fish flakes easily when tested with fork. Makes 4 servings.

MARINADES FOR FISH

Each marinade makes enough for 1 lb (500 g) fish fillets or steaks. For marinating and grilling times, follow the recipe for Grilled Mustard Dill Fish (p. 51).

TARRAGON LEMON MARINADE

1/4 cup	olive oil	50 mL
2 tsp	finely grated lemon rind	10 mL
1/4 cup	lemon juice	50 mL
1 tbsp	chopped fresh tarragon (or 2 tsp/10 mL dried)	15 mL
Pinch	each salt and pepper	Pinch

● In shallow dish, combine oil, lemon rind and juice, tarragon, salt and pepper. Makes 1/2 cup (125 mL).

TERIYAKI MARINADE

1/3 cup	orange juice	75 mL
1/4 cup	soy sauce	50 mL
2 tbsp	rice wine vinegar or cider vinegar	25 mL
1 tbsp	grated gingerroot	15 mL
1 tsp	sesame oil	5 mL
1	clove garlic, minced	1

● In shallow dish, combine orange juice, soy sauce, vinegar, ginger, oil and garlic. Makes 2/3 cup (150 mL).

Grilled Mustard Dill Fish ▲

1 lb	fish steaks or thick fillets	500 g
	MUSTARD DILL MARINADE	
1/4 cup	lemon juice	50 mL
2 tbsp	chopped fresh dill	25 mL
2 tbsp	olive oil	25 mL
2 tbsp	Dijon mustard	25 mL
Pinch	each salt and pepper	Pinch

● MUSTARD DILL MARINADE: In shallow dish, combine lemon juice, dill, oil, mustard, salt and pepper; add fish, turning to coat.

Cover and marinate in refrigerator for at least 45 minutes or up to 2 hours, turning occasionally.

● Reserving marinade, place fish on greased grill over medium-high heat; cover partially or completely for smokier flavor, if desired. Cook, turning and basting with marinade halfway through, for about 10 minutes per inch (2.5 cm) of thickness or until fish is opaque and flakes easily when tested with fork. Makes 4 servings.

Halibut is the catch of the day — meaty enough for the grill yet so mild in taste that it's a perfect match for a variety of herbs and spices. Serve with Leeks on the Grill (p. 77) and Mango Salsa (p. 70).

Garlicky Curry Skewered Fish

With a mild curry accent, everyday fish such as Boston bluefish takes on company airs. Round out the Asian flavors with Basmati rice.

1 lb	fish fillets, 1 inch (2.5 cm) thick	500 g
1	zucchini	1
Half	red onion	Half
1/3 cup	butter, melted	75 mL
1	clove garlic, minced	1
1 tsp	curry powder	5 mL
1/2 tsp	salt	2 mL
1/4 tsp	pepper	1 mL
4	cherry tomatoes	4

● Cut fillets into 1-inch (2.5 cm) cubes; pat dry. Slice zucchini into 1/4-inch (5 mm) thick slices. Cut onion into 4 quarters; separate layers. Alternately thread fish, zucchini and onion onto 4 skewers.

● Combine butter, garlic, curry powder, salt and pepper.

● Place skewers on greased grill over medium-high heat; cook, turning and brushing often with butter mixture, for 8 to 12 minutes or until fish flakes easily when tested with fork and vegetables are tender-crisp. Garnish with cherry tomato on end of each skewer. Makes 4 servings.

Grilled Pickerel Skewers

Thin strips of pickerel, threaded onto skewers and grilled to moist perfection, make a sophisticated summer supper — especially with the fresh tomato salsa. A rice pilaf and fresh summer greens are great menu mates.

1 lb	pickerel fillets	500 g
	Vegetable oil	
	Salt and pepper	
	Lemon Dill Mayonnaise or Tomato Chive Salsa (recipes follow)	

● Cut pickerel into 4- x 3/4-inch (10 x 2 cm) strips. Thread each strip onto skewer. Brush with oil; sprinkle with salt and pepper to taste.

● Place skewers on greased grill over medium heat; cook, carefully turning once, for about 5 minutes on each side or until fish flakes easily when tested with fork. Serve with Lemon Dill Mayonnaise or Tomato Chive Salsa. Makes 4 servings.

LEMON DILL MAYONNAISE		
1/3 cup	light mayonnaise	75 mL
1/3 cup	plain low-fat yogurt	75 mL
2 tbsp	chopped fresh dill	25 mL
1 tsp	grated lemon rind	5 mL
	Salt and pepper	

● In bowl, stir together mayonnaise, yogurt, dill, lemon rind, and salt and pepper to taste. Makes about 2/3 cup (150 mL).

TOMATO CHIVE SALSA		
1	ripe tomato, cored, seeded and diced	1
3 tbsp	chopped fresh chives or green onions	50 mL
1 tbsp	olive oil	15 mL
1/2 tsp	grated lemon rind	2 mL
2 tsp	lemon juice	10 mL
1/4 tsp	each salt and pepper	1 mL

● In bowl, gently stir together tomato, chives, oil, lemon rind and juice, salt and pepper. Makes about 1 cup (250 mL).

BARBECUING FISH AND SEAFOOD

Fish and seafood have distinct advantages on the grill: they cook quickly, have flavors enhanced by grilling and marry well with simple marinades, which keep them moist. The secret is simplicity. Don't overcook or turn any more than necessary. For best results, grill fish that is at least 1 inch (2.5 cm) thick. Thin or tender-fleshed fish is best cooked in a greased grill basket or wrapped in foil.

Salade Niçoise

6	small new potatoes	6
1 cup	thin green beans, trimmed	250 mL
1 cup	flaked grilled fish	250 mL
1	sweet green pepper, cut into strips	1
2	tomatoes, quartered	2
4	hard-cooked eggs, cut into wedges	4
1/2 cup	thinly sliced red onion	125 mL
1/4 cup	pitted black olives	50 mL
	NIÇOISE VINAIGRETTE	
1/2 cup	olive oil	125 mL
1/4 cup	chopped fresh basil	50 mL
1/4 cup	red wine vinegar	50 mL
2 tbsp	chopped fresh parsley	25 mL
2 tsp	dry mustard	10 mL
1/2 tsp	salt	2 mL
1/4 tsp	pepper	1 mL

● NIÇOISE VINAIGRETTE: In jar with tight-fitting lid, combine oil, basil, vinegar, parsley, mustard, salt and pepper; shake well. Set aside.

● Scrub potatoes but do not peel; cook in saucepan of boiling water for 15 minutes or just until tender. Remove with slotted spoon; cut into halves or quarters while still warm.

● Add beans to boiling water; cook for 3 minutes or until tender-crisp. Refresh under cold water and pat dry.

● Mound fish in center of serving platter. Using same bowl, separately toss potatoes, beans and green pepper with about three-quarters of the vinaigrette. Arrange each, after tossing, around fish like spokes of wheel.

● Add tomatoes, eggs, onion and olives to platter in same pattern. Drizzle remaining vinaigrette over fish and tomatoes. Makes 4 servings.

Freshly grilled or leftover grilled fish gives a new twist to a classic summer salad from the south of France. There, the salad is made with canned tuna — an excellent stand-by ingredient that lets you serve up this sunny salad year-round.

Warm Paella Salad

3 cups	chicken stock	750 mL
1/2 tsp	saffron threads (or 1/4 tsp/1 mL powdered saffron) or turmeric	2 mL
1-1/2 cups	long grain parboiled rice	375 mL
3 tbsp	olive oil	45 mL
1	large sweet red pepper, chopped	1
1	large clove garlic, minced	1
2	green onions, chopped	2
1 cup	frozen peas, thawed	250 mL
1/4 cup	chopped fresh parsley	50 mL
3 tbsp	lemon juice	45 mL
1 tsp	salt	5 mL
1/2 tsp	pepper	2 mL
2 cups	flaked grilled fish	500 mL

● In saucepan, bring stock and saffron to boil; stir in rice. Reduce heat to low; cover and cook for 20 minutes or until rice is tender and liquid is absorbed.

● Meanwhile, in large skillet, heat oil over medium-high heat; cook red pepper, stirring often, for 3 minutes or until softened. Add garlic and onions; cook for 2 minutes.

● Stir in peas, parsley, lemon juice, salt and pepper. Add to rice along with fish; toss gently. Makes 6 servings.

Paella is a large saffron-scented rice dish studded with chorizo sausage, chicken, mussels and peppers. Here's a lighter salad version using freshly grilled or leftover fish. It's ideal for summer picnics and suppers.

APPETIZER SCALLOPS

Cook a refreshing seafood appetizer on the barbecue to take the edge off appetites while waiting for the main course.

● In bowl, marinate about 1 lb (500 g) large scallops in 2 tbsp (25 mL) vegetable oil, 1 tbsp (15 mL) lemon juice and 1/2 tsp (2 mL) liquid smoke for 30 minutes; thread onto skewers. Place on greased grill over high heat; cook just until opaque.

Lemon Rainbow Trout

No bones means no fuss when eating fish. Add that to trout's moistness, pleasing flavor and availability — and it's easy to understand why this farm-raised fish has become so popular.

2 tbsp	lemon juice	25 mL
1 tbsp	chopped fresh dill	15 mL
1 tsp	vegetable oil	5 mL
3	cloves garlic, minced	3
1/2 tsp	pepper	2 mL
1/4 tsp	salt	1 mL
4	rainbow trout fillets (each 5 oz/150 g)	4

● In small bowl, whisk together lemon juice, dill, oil, garlic, pepper and salt.

● Place trout, skin side down, on greased grill over low heat; brush with half of the lemon mixture. Cook, covered, for 8 minutes.

● Turn fish over; brush with remaining lemon mixture. Cook, covered, for 4 to 5 minutes or until fish flakes easily when tested with fork. Makes 4 servings.

Mussels with Lemon Garlic Butter

As an appetizer, four to six mussels per person are enough. For a main course, plan on eight to a dozen per person.

2 lb	mussels	1 kg
1/2 cup	white wine or water	125 mL
	Lemon Garlic Butter (recipe follows)	

● Scrub mussels under cold water, removing any beards. Discard any that do not close when tapped.

● Divide mussels between two 22- x 18-inch (55 x 45 cm) pieces of heavy-duty foil; sprinkle with wine. Loosely wrap foil over mussels, sealing tightly.

● Place on grill over high heat; cook for 5 to 7 minutes or until mussels open. Discard any that do not open. Serve with Lemon Garlic Butter for dipping. Makes 4 servings.

LEMON GARLIC BUTTER		
1/2 cup	butter	125 mL
3 tbsp	lemon juice	50 mL
1	clove garlic, minced	1

● In saucepan, melt butter; stir in lemon juice and garlic. Makes 2/3 cup (150 mL).

Lime-Grilled Lobster

Frozen lobster tails are the handiest lobster to enjoy in this superb grill. Thaw lobster by placing the package in cold water.

5 lb	cooked lobster tails (in shell)	2.2 kg
2 tsp	grated lime rind	10 mL
1/2 cup	lime juice	125 mL
1/4 cup	olive oil	50 mL
1/4 tsp	pepper	1 mL
1/2 cup	butter, melted	125 mL
	Lime wedges	

● Split lobster tails lengthwise; place, cracked side up, in shallow dish.

● Whisk together lime rind, 1/3 cup (75 mL) of the lime juice, oil and pepper; drizzle into cracked portion of lobster. Cover and marinate in refrigerator for 30 minutes, turning occasionally.

● Reserving marinade, place lobster, cracked side down, on greased grill over high heat; cook, brushing cracked side twice with marinade, for 5 to 6 minutes or until heated through.

● Stir remaining lime juice into butter; serve as dipping sauce. Garnish lobster with lime wedges. Makes 4 servings.

Garlic Seafood Skewers ▼

1	each salmon and halibut fillet, skinned (each about 6 oz/175 g)	1
8	large fresh shrimp (about 6 oz/175 g)	8
4	large fresh scallops (about 6 oz/175 g)	4
	MARINADE	
3 tbsp	olive oil	50 mL
1 tbsp	white wine vinegar	15 mL
3	large cloves garlic, minced	3
1 tbsp	chopped fresh thyme	15 mL
1/4 tsp	each dry mustard, salt and pepper	1 mL

● Cut salmon and halibut into 1-inch (2.5 cm) cubes. Peel and devein shrimp.

● Onto each of 4 skewers, thread shrimp, piece of halibut, piece of salmon, scallop and shrimp. Arrange in single layer in shallow glass dish.

● MARINADE: Whisk together oil, vinegar, garlic, thyme, mustard, salt and pepper; pour over skewers. Cover and marinate at room temperature for 30 minutes.

● Reserving marinade, place skewers on greased grill over medium-high heat; cook, turning once and brushing with marinade, for 8 to 10 minutes or until fish flakes easily when tested with fork and scallops are opaque. Makes 4 servings.

E*legant seafood skewers are the perfect solution when you need an effortless special-occasion dish from the grill. If you prefer, substitute monkfish, swordfish or tuna for the salmon and the halibut.*

Crisp Grilled Squid ▼

Calamari, *deep-fried squid, is one of today's popular finger foods. Believe it or not, squid is even more succulent on the barbecue, especially with a squirt of lemon.*

1 lb	squid, cleaned	500 g
3 tbsp	olive oil	50 mL
1/2 cup	dry bread crumbs	125 mL
1 tsp	salt	5 mL
1/2 tsp	pepper	2 mL
	Lemon wedges	

● Cut pouches down one long side of squid and open out; cut lengthwise into 3 sections. Score crosshatch on outside of each section.

● Place squid and tentacles in bowl and toss with oil; marinate for 30 minutes. Remove and shake off excess oil.

● Thread squid lengthwise onto short soaked wooden skewers. On plate, mix together bread crumbs, salt and pepper. Place squid in mixture, turning to lightly coat; shake off excess.

● Place on greased grill over medium-high heat; cook, turning once, for 8 to 12 minutes or until bread crumbs are crisp and squid is firm. Serve with lemon wedges. Makes 8 servings.

TIP: To clean squid, separate tentacles from pouch, just below eyes. Remove long, rigid quill and remaining body parts. Pull off skin. Cut off tentacles above eyes, squeezing out bony beak if it remains; discard eyes and beak. Wash pouch and tentacles.

Curried Shrimp for Two

1/2 lb	shrimp	250 g
	MARINADE	
1/2 tsp	grated lime rind	2 mL
2 tbsp	lime juice	25 mL
2 tbsp	chopped fresh coriander or parsley	25 mL
1 tbsp	granulated sugar	15 mL
1 tbsp	olive oil	15 mL
1	clove garlic, minced	1
1 tsp	curry powder	5 mL
1/4 tsp	each ground cumin and dried coriander	1 mL
Pinch	each salt and pepper	Pinch
1	small zucchini	1
1	small sweet red pepper	1

● Peel and devein shrimp, leaving tails attached; set aside.

● MARINADE: In bowl, whisk together lime rind and juice, fresh coriander, sugar, oil, garlic, curry powder, cumin, dried coriander, salt and pepper. Gently stir in shrimp, stirring to coat well. Cover and marinate at room temperature for 30 minutes.

● Meanwhile, cut zucchini and red pepper into bite-size chunks.

● Reserving marinade, alternately thread shrimp, zucchini and red pepper onto skewers, threading shrimp lengthwise through top and tail end. Place on greased grill over medium-high heat; cook, turning once and basting with marinade, for 8 to 10 minutes or until shrimp are bright pink. Makes 2 servings.

Very quick, very easy — and very good! Shrimp with zucchini and sweet red pepper make a stylish summertime supper.

Barbecued Whitefish

1	whitefish (about 2-1/4 lb/1.125 kg), cleaned	1
1 cup	loosely packed fresh herbs	250 mL
3 tbsp	vegetable oil	50 mL
2 tbsp	dry white wine or vermouth	25 mL
4 tsp	chopped fresh herbs	20 mL
1/4 tsp	pepper	1 mL
	Salt	
	Lemon wedges	

● In shallow glass dish, combine oil, wine, chopped herbs and pepper; add fish, turning to coat. Cover and marinate in refrigerator for 2 hours, turning several times.

● Reserving any marinade, place fish in greased wire basket and close basket. Place on grill over medium-high heat; cook, turning once and basting with marinade occasionally, for 10 minutes per inch (2.5 cm) of thickness or until fish flakes easily when tested with fork. Season with salt to taste. Place on platter and garnish with lemon. Makes 4 servings.

● Rinse fish; pat dry inside and out. Cut four 1/4-inch (5 mm) deep slashes on the diagonal across each side of fish. Stuff fresh herbs into cavity.

Whitefish is an excellent choice for cooking on the grill. Its skin becomes crisp and tasty, and its flesh moist and easy to lift off the bones. It also marries beautifully with fresh herbs such as parsley, tarragon, dill or basil. This recipe suits other fish of the same size such as lake trout, pickerel, salmon trout and small whole salmon.

TIP: To serve whole fish, use knife to slit fish along backbone; peel off skin. Ease wide-bladed fish server under fillet, keeping blade as close to bones as possible; lift fillet neatly off bones. Turn fish over and repeat with other fillet.

Good-Time Burgers

For a crowd pleaser, you can't beat thick and juicy grill-marked burgers. Why not flip pork, lamb, chicken, turkey or tofu patties onto the barbecue for a delicious change of taste?

Creole Superburger ▶

O*ne big patty, drenched with a zesty tomato sauce and sandwiched in a round loaf of crusty Italian bread, is a fun idea for a barbecue party. Cut into wedges to serve along with corn on the cob and summery greens.*

4	eggs	4
2 cups	fresh bread crumbs	500 mL
1	small onion, minced	1
1	stalk celery, minced	1
Half	sweet red or green pepper, minced	Half
3 tbsp	chopped fresh coriander or parsley	50 mL
3	green onions, minced	3
1 tbsp	Dijon mustard	15 mL
1 tbsp	Worcestershire sauce	15 mL
2	cloves garlic, minced	2
1 tsp	minced gingerroot	5 mL
1 tsp	salt	5 mL
1/4 tsp	pepper	1 mL
2 lb	ground beef	1 kg
1	round Italian bread (about 10 inches/25 cm)	1
	Creole Sauce (recipe follows)	

● In bowl, beat eggs; mix in bread crumbs, onion, celery, red pepper, coriander, green onions, mustard, Worcestershire sauce, garlic, ginger, salt and pepper; mix in beef. Shape on springform pan base into 9-inch (23 cm) patty.

● Slide patty onto greased grill over medium heat; cook, turning once, for about 20 minutes or until no longer pink inside.

● Slice bread in half into 2 rounds; place burger on bottom half. Spoon about 2 cups (500 mL) Creole Sauce over burger. Top with remaining bread. Cut into wedges. Serve with remaining sauce. Makes 8 servings.

CREOLE SAUCE		
2 tbsp	olive oil	25 mL
1	onion, chopped	1
3	cloves garlic, minced	3
1	hot banana pepper, finely chopped	1
2	stalks celery, chopped	2
1	each sweet green and red pepper, chopped	1
1 cup	tomato sauce	250 mL
1 cup	water	250 mL
1/2 cup	ketchup	125 mL
1/2 tsp	hot pepper sauce	2 mL
	Salt and pepper	

● In deep skillet, heat oil over medium-high heat; cook onion, garlic and hot pepper for about 2 minutes or until softened. Add celery and sweet peppers; cook for 5 minutes.

● Add tomato sauce, water and ketchup; bring to boil. Reduce heat and simmer gently for 15 to 20 minutes or until thickened. Season with hot pepper sauce, and salt and pepper to taste. *(Sauce can be cooled, covered and refrigerated for up to 5 days.)* Makes 3 cups (750 mL).

TIP: To turn a superburger, slip a springform pan base under burger, place another springform base or baking sheet on top, then flip and slide burger back onto grill.

Your Basic Burger

For a really tasty burger that can stand on its own without condiments, here's how you do it. Add herbs or a dash of hot pepper sauce to the recipe, if you like.

1	egg	1
1/4 cup	dry bread crumbs	50 mL
1/4 cup	finely chopped onion	50 mL
2 tbsp	water	25 mL
2 tsp	Dijon mustard	10 mL
1	clove garlic, minced	1
1/2 tsp	salt	2 mL
1/4 tsp	pepper	1 mL
1/4 tsp	Worcestershire sauce	1 mL
1 lb	ground beef	500 g
4	hamburger buns	4

● In bowl, beat egg; mix in bread crumbs, onion, water, mustard, garlic, salt, pepper and Worcestershire sauce. Mix in beef; shape into four 3/4-inch (2 cm) thick patties.

● Place on greased grill over medium heat; cook, turning once, for 10 to 12 minutes or until no longer pink inside. Sandwich in buns. Makes 4 servings.

TIP: The added water helps keep burgers juicy, especially when well done.

Greek Beef Burgers

Tuck these crusty burgers along with sliced tomatoes, red onions and cucumber into warmed pitas and spoon in some of the refreshing Yogurt Mint Sauce. A tabbouleh salad studded with pine nuts and currants rounds out the meal perfectly.

2	large cloves garlic, quartered	2
1 tsp	salt	5 mL
6	green onions, coarsely chopped	6
1/3 cup	packed fresh mint	75 mL
1/4 cup	snipped fresh dill	50 mL
1	each sweet red and green pepper, coarsely chopped	1
2 lb	ground beef	1 kg
1 tbsp	grated lemon rind	15 mL
2 tbsp	lemon juice	25 mL
1 tbsp	dried oregano	15 mL
1/2 tsp	each cinnamon, ground cumin and pepper	2 mL
4	pita breads, warmed	4
	Yogurt Mint Sauce (recipe follows)	

● In food processor, purée garlic and salt until pastelike. Add green onions, mint and dill; chop until minced. Add red and green pepper; purée until finely ground.

● In bowl, mix together ground sweet pepper mixture, beef, lemon rind and juice, oregano, cinnamon, cumin and pepper; shape into eight 3/4-inch (2 cm) thick patties.

● Place on greased grill over medium heat; cook, turning once, for 10 to 12 minutes or until no longer pink inside.

● Cut pitas in half; open to form pockets. Insert burger into each; drizzle with Yogurt Mint Sauce. Makes 8 servings.

YOGURT MINT SAUCE		
1/2 tsp	salt	2 mL
2	small cloves garlic, quartered	2
1/4 cup	packed fresh mint	50 mL
2 cups	plain yogurt	500 mL
Pinch	granulated sugar	Pinch

● In food processor, purée salt and garlic until pastelike. Add mint; using on/off motion, mince finely, scraping down bowl twice. Combine with yogurt and sugar. *(Sauce can be refrigerated for up to 8 hours.)* Makes 2 cups (500 mL).

GROUND BEEF FOR BURGERS

Lean and medium ground beef are both suitable for burgers. Although lean is lower in fat, fat does drip off medium ground beef during grilling — and medium is often on sale, especially during the barbecue season.

Salsa Burgers

1	egg	1
3/4 cup	chunky salsa	175 mL
1/2 cup	dry bread crumbs	125 mL
1	onion, finely chopped	1
1 tbsp	Dijon mustard	15 mL
2 tsp	chili powder	10 mL
1/2 tsp	each salt and pepper	2 mL
2 lb	ground beef	1 kg
8	hamburger buns	8

● In large bowl, beat egg; mix in salsa, bread crumbs, onion, mustard, chili powder, salt and pepper. Mix in beef; shape into eight 3/4-inch (2 cm) thick patties.

● Place on greased grill over medium-high heat; cook, turning once, for 10 minutes or until no longer pink inside. Sandwich in buns. Makes 8 servings.

A good dose of salsa mixed in with the meat guarantees a moist and juicy burger every time.

TIP: To get a head start on easy weeknight suppers or weekends away at the cottage or camping, make up a stack of burger patties, layering each between waxed paper, and freeze in freezer bags or airtight containers for up to 1 month.

Pizza Burgers

1	egg	1
1/4 cup	dry bread crumbs	50 mL
1/4 cup	finely chopped onion	50 mL
1/2 cup	tomato sauce	125 mL
1/4 cup	sliced black olives	50 mL
1	clove garlic, minced	1
1-1/2 tsp	each dried basil and oregano	7 mL
1/2 tsp	salt	2 mL
1/4 tsp	pepper	1 mL
1 lb	ground beef	500 g
4	slices each sweet green pepper and tomato	4
1 cup	shredded mozzarella cheese	250 mL
4	hamburger buns	4

● In bowl, beat egg; mix in bread crumbs, onion, 2 tbsp (25 mL) of the tomato sauce, half of the olives, garlic, basil, oregano, salt and pepper. Mix in beef; shape into four 3/4-inch (2 cm) thick patties.

● Place on greased grill over medium heat; cook for 7 minutes. Turn patties and cook for 4 minutes.

● Pour remaining tomato sauce evenly over patties; top each with green pepper and tomato slice. Divide remaining olives among patties; sprinkle with cheese.

● Cover and cook for about 3 minutes or until meat is no longer pink inside and cheese is melted. Sandwich in buns. Makes 4 servings.

Cheeseburgers with an Italian touch! To add to the flavor, serve the patties between rounds or squares of focaccia.

Caesar Burgers

Even if you're a "No anchovies on my pizza" person, don't leave the anchovy paste out here as it mellows wonderfully with the other Caesar flavors — garlic, lemon and Worcestershire.

1	egg	1
1-1/4 lb	ground beef	625 g
1/4 cup	freshly grated Parmesan cheese	50 mL
2 tbsp	lemon juice	25 mL
1 tbsp	anchovy paste	15 mL
1 tbsp	Worcestershire sauce	15 mL
1/4 tsp	pepper	1 mL
2 tbsp	olive oil	25 mL
1	clove garlic, minced	1
4	kaiser rolls, halved	4
4	leaves romaine lettuce	4

● In bowl, beat egg; mix in beef, half of the Parmesan cheese, lemon juice, anchovy paste, Worcestershire sauce and pepper. Shape into four 3/4-inch (2 cm) thick patties.

● Place on greased grill over medium-high heat; cook, turning once, for 10 to 12 minutes or until no longer pink inside.

● Meanwhile, combine oil and garlic; brush over cut side of rolls. Place on grill and toast.

● Place burgers on rolls; sprinkle with remaining cheese and top with romaine. Makes 4 servings.

Apple-Stuffed Pork Burgers

Use lean ground pork in this delicious twist on a summer burger. A tangy cabbage and carrot slaw goes well with the apple filling inside the sage-and-mustard patties.

1 tbsp	butter	15 mL
1	small onion, minced	1
1	small apple, peeled, cored and minced	1
1/2 cup	dry bread crumbs	125 mL
2 tbsp	water	25 mL
1 tsp	Dijon mustard	5 mL
1/2 tsp	each salt, pepper and dried sage	2 mL
1 lb	lean ground pork	500 g
4	hamburger buns	4

● In skillet, melt butter over medium heat; cook onion and apple for about 4 minutes or until softened.

● Add half of the bread crumbs, the water and mustard; cook for 1 minute. Add half of the salt, pepper and sage.

● In bowl, combine pork with remaining salt, pepper and sage; shape into 8 thin patties. Mound apple mixture on top of 4 patties, leaving 1/2-inch (1 cm) border; cover with remaining patties, pressing firmly to seal in apple mixture. Coat patties with remaining crumbs.

● Place on greased grill over medium heat; cook, turning once, for 16 to 20 minutes or until no longer pink inside. Sandwich in buns. Makes 4 servings.

FOR A BETTER BURGER

● Add liquid, such as water or milk, to the ground meat mixture to ensure a juicy burger.

● When forming patties or meatballs, press ingredients together lightly. If the mixture is too compact, the cooked meat will be tough.

● Burgers always taste better on toasted buns. For extra flavor, spread buns with Dijon mustard, or mayonnaise mixed with crushed garlic and a pinch of cayenne pepper.

● There's more to burgers than plain hamburger buns. For a change, try whole wheat buns, kaiser rolls, Portuguese pada buns or pita breads. There's also focaccia — the round ones are best, sliced horizontally — or thick baguettes, cut into wide slices and hinged open to hold the patty. Some people like to wrap a burger in a warm tortilla, but you have to watch for drips. Forget about bagels for burgers, though — there's that hole!

Turkey Burgers with Kiwi Salsa ▲

1	egg	1
1-1/4 lb	ground turkey or chicken	625 g
1/3 cup	dry bread crumbs	75 mL
3 tbsp	milk or cream	50 mL
1/2 tsp	salt	2 mL
1/4 tsp	pepper	1 mL
6	hamburger buns	6
	Kiwi Salsa (recipe follows)	

● In bowl, beat egg; mix in turkey, bread crumbs, milk, salt and pepper. Form into six 3/4-inch (2 cm) thick patties.

● Place on greased grill over medium heat; cook, turning once, for about 10 minutes or until no longer pink inside. Place in buns; spoon on Kiwi Salsa. Makes 6 servings.

	KIWI SALSA	
2	kiwifruit, peeled and diced	2
1/2 cup	diced red onion	125 mL
2 tbsp	lime juice	25 mL
2 tsp	packed brown sugar	10 mL
1/2 tsp	dried oregano	2 mL

● In bowl, stir together kiwifruit, onion, lime juice, sugar and oregano. Makes 1-1/2 cups (375 mL).

A freshly made salsa livens up burgers, but they're also delicious with store-bought salsa or your favorite relish.

Grilled Fillet Burgers ▼

A *firm-fleshed fish such as salmon, halibut, shark, tuna, monkfish or Boston bluefish is best right on the grill. If fillets have skin, grill skin side down, then turn carefully with a wide lifter. Remove skin and brush with remaining juice mixture.*

1 tbsp	lemon juice	15 mL
1 tbsp	vegetable oil	15 mL
1 tsp	dry mustard	5 mL
1/4 tsp	salt	1 mL
Pinch	pepper	Pinch
1 lb	fish fillets	500 g
	Lettuce	
2	sweet yellow peppers, roasted (see TIP, this page)	2
4	whole wheat sesame hamburger buns	4
	Minced dill pickle	
	LIGHT TARTAR SAUCE	
1/2 cup	plain low-fat yogurt	125 mL
1/4 cup	minced dill pickle	50 mL
2 tbsp	light mayonnaise	25 mL
Pinch	cayenne pepper	Pinch

● In small bowl, combine lemon juice, oil, mustard, salt and pepper; brush half over fish.

● Place fish on greased grill over medium-high heat; cook, turning once and brushing with remaining juice mixture, for 10 minutes per inch (2.5 cm) of thickness or until fish flakes easily when tested with fork.

● LIGHT TARTAR SAUCE: In bowl, combine yogurt, pickle, mayonnaise and cayenne.

● Place lettuce, peppers and fish on bottom half of buns; top with dollop of sauce. Sprinkle with pickle and top with remaining bun halves. Makes 4 servings.

TIP: To roast sweet peppers, cook on greased grill over medium-high heat, turning often, for 20 to 25 minutes or until charred. Let cool slightly; peel, seed and cut into quarters.

(from left) Grilled Fillet Burger, Chicken Burger Provençal and Mediterranean Burger.

Mediterranean Burgers ◄

1	egg	1
1/4 cup	dry bread crumbs	50 mL
1/4 cup	finely chopped onion	50 mL
2 tbsp	chopped fresh mint	25 mL
1/2 tsp	grated lemon rind	2 mL
2 tbsp	lemon juice	25 mL
2 tsp	Dijon mustard	10 mL
1	clove garlic, minced	1
1/2 tsp	each salt and ground cumin	2 mL
1/4 tsp	pepper	1 mL
1 lb	ground beef	500 g
4	slices tomato	4
4	whole wheat sesame hamburger buns	4

QUICK CUCUMBER PICKLES		
1/3 cup	white vinegar	75 mL
1 tbsp	granulated sugar	15 mL
Pinch	each salt and pepper	Pinch
Half	English cucumber, thinly sliced	Half
1 tsp	chopped fresh mint	5 mL

● QUICK CUCUMBER PICKLES: In saucepan, combine vinegar, sugar, salt and pepper; bring to boil, stirring. Reduce heat and simmer for 2 minutes; add cucumber and mint. Chill for 1 hour.

● In bowl, beat egg; mix in bread crumbs, onion, mint, lemon rind and juice, mustard, garlic, salt, cumin and pepper. Mix in beef; shape into four 3/4-inch (2 cm) thick patties.

● Place on greased grill over medium heat; cook, turning once, for 12 to 14 minutes or until no longer pink inside. Sandwich burgers, tomato and cucumber pickles in buns. Makes 4 servings.

Mint is typical of the fresh tastes of the eastern Mediterranean. All the flavors in this burger work just as well with another popular meat from this region — lean ground lamb.

Chicken Burgers Provençal ◄

1	egg	1
1/4 cup	dry bread crumbs	50 mL
1/4 cup	finely chopped onion	50 mL
2	cloves garlic, minced	2
2 tbsp	water	25 mL
2 tsp	Dijon mustard	10 mL
1 tsp	chopped fresh rosemary	5 mL
1/2 tsp	salt	2 mL
1/4 tsp	pepper	1 mL
1 lb	ground chicken or turkey	500 g
1	small red onion	1
2 tsp	olive oil	10 mL
2	sweet red peppers, roasted (see Tip, p. 64)	2
4	whole wheat sesame hamburger buns	4

GARLIC SAUCE		
1/2 cup	light sour cream	125 mL
1 tbsp	light mayonnaise	15 mL
1	clove garlic, minced	1

● GARLIC SAUCE: In small bowl, stir together sour cream, mayonnaise and garlic.

● In bowl, beat egg; mix in bread crumbs, onion, garlic, water, mustard, rosemary, salt and pepper. Mix in chicken; shape into four 3/4-inch (2 cm) thick patties.

● Place on greased grill over medium heat; cook, turning once, for 12 to 14 minutes (about 20 minutes for turkey) or until no longer pink inside.

● Meanwhile, slice red onion; brush with oil. Grill for 6 minutes or until tender and golden, turning halfway through. Sandwich burgers, 2 pieces of red pepper and onions in buns; add dollop of garlic sauce. Makes 4 servings.

TIP: Use the garlic sauce on any basic burger. You can flavor the sour cream/mayonnaise mixture with your favorite herb, chopped green onions or tangy green relish.

Equally delicious with ground lamb, these burgers zing with rosemary and garlic — the lusty flavors of southern France.

Lamb Burgers

If ground lamb is not available where you shop, ask the butcher to oblige — the taste is well worth the effort! For a great summer party appetizer, tuck mini versions of these burgers into little pita breads.

1 tbsp	vegetable oil	15 mL
1	onion, minced	1
1	clove garlic, minced	1
2 tbsp	milk	25 mL
1/4 cup	fresh bread crumbs	50 mL
1	egg, beaten	1
1 tbsp	chopped fresh coriander	15 mL
1/2 tsp	each ground cumin and salt	2 mL
1/4 tsp	pepper	1 mL
1 lb	ground lamb	500 g
3	pita breads	3
	Yogurt Mint Sauce (recipe, p.60)	

● In skillet, heat oil over medium heat; cook onion and garlic for 3 minutes or until softened. Let cool.

● Meanwhile, in bowl, add milk to bread crumbs; add onion mixture, egg, coriander, cumin, salt and pepper. Mix in lamb; form into six 1/2-inch (1 cm) thick patties.

● Place on greased grill over medium heat; cook, turning once, for 12 to 14 minutes or until no longer pink inside.

● Cut pitas in half; open to form pockets. Insert burger into each; drizzle with Yogurt Mint Sauce. Makes 6 servings.

Herbed Parmesan Chicken Burgers

If authentic Parmesan cheese (Parmigiano Reggiano) is not available, avoid pre-grated imitations and choose instead a shredded old Cheddar or Gruyère.

1	egg	1
1	clove garlic, minced	1
1/2 cup	dry bread crumbs	125 mL
1/2 cup	chopped green onions	125 mL
2 tbsp	chopped fresh parsley	25 mL
1 tbsp	freshly grated Parmesan cheese	15 mL
3/4 tsp	each dried basil and oregano	4 mL
1/2 tsp	salt	2 mL
1/4 tsp	pepper	1 mL
1 lb	ground chicken	500 g
4	hamburger buns	4

● In bowl, beat egg; mix in garlic, bread crumbs, green onions, parsley, Parmesan cheese, basil, oregano, salt and pepper. Mix in chicken; form into four 1/2-inch (1 cm) thick patties.

● Place on greased grill over medium heat; cook, turning once, for 12 to 14 minutes or until no longer pink inside. Sandwich in buns. Makes 4 servings.

HOT DIGGITY DOGS!

Choose your Dog

With new varieties of wieners packing the processed meat cases every day, there's now a dog for everyone.

● Choose turkey, veal and chicken wieners, as well as the usual beef and pork. There are lower-fat varieties, too.

● For vegetarians, there's a choice between tofu and vegetable-based wieners.

● And don't forget all those sausages that taste great wrapped in a bun.

● There's a bun for everybody, too. Wrap wieners in pita bread, torpedo or sub buns, even focaccia.

Dog Dress-ups

● PORCUPINE DOG: Snip along both sides of wiener at even intervals before barbecuing.

● CIRCLES: Score wieners every 1/2 inch (1 cm) along one side, cutting almost through; wieners become circles when grilled. Serve in hamburger buns.

● PIG IN A BLANKET: Cut focaccia bread into pieces large enough to wrap around a barbecued wiener.

● DOGGY BOBS: Cut wiener into 3 or 4 large pieces. Thread onto metal skewer alternately with small parboiled potatoes. Barbecue until wiener and potatoes are crisp and golden.

Tofu Burgers in Pita Pockets

1 lb	firm tofu	500 g
1	egg yolk	1
1/3 cup	dry bread crumbs	75 mL
3 tbsp	finely chopped green onion	50 mL
1 tbsp	soy sauce	15 mL
1 tsp	Dijon mustard	5 mL
1/4 tsp	each ground cumin, dried marjoram and salt	1 mL
Pinch	pepper	Pinch
2	pita breads	2

● Place tofu on plate; place another plate on top and weigh down with heavy can. Let stand for 15 minutes to remove excess moisture; drain.

● In bowl, mash tofu with fork; mix in egg yolk, bread crumbs, onion, soy sauce, mustard, cumin, marjoram, salt and pepper. Shape into four 1/2-inch (1 cm) thick patties.

● Place on greased grill over medium-high heat; cook, turning once, for 10 to 12 minutes or until golden brown.

● Cut pitas in half and open to form pockets; insert tofu burger into each pocket. Makes 4 servings.

TIP: Use firm tofu for this recipe. Regular tofu will be too soft to barbecue, and extra-firm tofu will not hold together as well.

The Oriental flavors that go so well with tofu are nicely complemented by alfalfa sprouts and thinly sliced cucumbers piled into a warmed pita pocket along with the burger.

Reuben Burger Melts

1	egg	1
1/3 cup	chopped fresh parsley	75 mL
1/4 cup	dry bread crumbs	50 mL
1/4 cup	finely chopped onion	50 mL
2 tbsp	water	25 mL
2 tbsp	Dijon mustard	25 mL
2	cloves garlic, minced	2
1/2 tsp	salt	2 mL
1/4 tsp	pepper	1 mL
1 lb	lean ground pork	500 g
4	slices Swiss cheese	4
1 cup	sauerkraut, rinsed and drained	250 mL
2	dill pickles, sliced	2
4	slices rye bread	4

● In bowl, beat egg; mix in parsley, bread crumbs, onion, water, 2 tsp (10 mL) of the mustard, garlic, salt and pepper. Mix in pork; shape into four 3/4-inch (2 cm) thick patties.

● Place on greased grill over medium heat; cook for 8 minutes. Turn and cook for 5 minutes.

● Top each patty with cheese, sauerkraut and pickles; cover and cook for 3 minutes or until meat is no longer pink inside and cheese is melted.

● Meanwhile, grill bread for 2 to 3 minutes per side or until toasted; spread with remaining mustard. Place patties on bread. Makes 4 servings.

Instead of hamburger buns, these sauerkraut-topped burgers are sitting pretty on toasted dark rye bread. Serve open-faced, with knife and fork — or toast four extra slices of rye bread to go on top.

PLAY IT SAFE WITH BURGERS

● Check labels on ground meats in supermarkets to ensure that meat has been ground the day of purchase. Use within one day.

● Rare is a burger no-no. Always cook burgers until no longer pink inside. Ground meat can host harmful bacteria that are destroyed only by cooking the meat right through.

● Thaw frozen patties completely in the refrigerator before cooking in order to prevent charring the meat on the outside before it's cooked inside.

Saucy Toppers

What you lavish on a burger, mop on chicken or brush on a chop makes all the taste difference in the world. Here's our pick of the very best salsas, relishes and barbecue sauces.

Peppy Salsa ▶

*T*oday's crowd is passing up ketchup for a hit of salsa on their burgers — and for good reason. Salsa has less sugar than ketchup, and its spiciness is in tune with our more adventurous palates. Here's how to put up a summer and winter's supply.

1/2 lb	jalapeño peppers	250 g
8 cups	coarsely chopped peeled tomatoes	2 L
3 cups	chopped seeded Cubanelle, Anaheim or sweet banana peppers	750 mL
2 cups	chopped onions	500 mL
2 cups	cider vinegar	500 mL
1 cup	each chopped sweet red and yellow peppers	250 mL
4	cloves garlic, minced	4
1	can (5-1/2 oz/156 mL) tomato paste	1
2 tbsp	granulated sugar	25 mL
1 tbsp	salt	15 mL
2 tsp	paprika	10 mL
1 tsp	dried oregano	5 mL
1/4 cup	chopped fresh coriander	50 mL

● On plastic cutting board and wearing rubber gloves, cut jalapeño peppers in half; discard ribs and seeds. Chop finely to make 1 cup (250 mL).

● In large heavy nonaluminum saucepan, combine jalapeños, tomatoes, Cubanelle peppers, onions, vinegar, sweet peppers, garlic, tomato paste, sugar, salt, paprika and oregano; bring to boil.

● Reduce heat to medium-low; simmer, stirring often, for 1 hour or until thickened. To test thickness, place 1 tbsp (15 mL) salsa on plate and tilt plate; salsa should flow slowly in one stream. Add coriander; cook for 5 minutes.

● Pour into hot sterilized canning jars, leaving 1/2-inch (1 cm) headspace. Seal with prepared lids and screw on bands. Process in boiling water bath for 20 minutes (see Preserving Basics, p. 73). Makes 11 cups (2.75 L).

TIPS:
● For a fiery-hot salsa, use small Scotch bonnet peppers or long thin red chili peppers instead of the jalapeños. For a milder version, substitute sweet peppers.
● If any jars do not seal properly, refrigerate to use within 3 weeks.
● To peel a large quantity of tomatoes, place tomatoes in heatproof bowl or basin. Cover with boiling water and let stand for 30 to 60 seconds or until tomato skins loosen. Drain; rinse with cold water to prevent cooking, then peel.

THE FRESH NEW TASTE OF SALSA

"Salsa" is Spanish for sauce. Originally a chunky relish to top tacos, tortillas and nachos, it now includes all kinds of fresh or cooked fruit and vegetable combinations. There's usually a sharp acid ingredient (lime or lemon juice or vinegar) plus herbs such as coriander or rosemary. Low-fat and fresh-tasting, salsas are catching on all over North America.

Tomato Rosemary Salsa

Serve with any grilled lamb, especially chops.

1	large tomato, seeded and diced	1
3 tbsp	finely chopped green onion	50 mL
1 tbsp	olive oil	15 mL
2 tsp	chopped fresh rosemary	10 mL
2 tsp	red wine vinegar	10 mL
1/4 tsp	each salt and pepper	1 mL

● In bowl, gently stir together tomato, onion, olive oil, rosemary, vinegar, salt and pepper. Let stand at room temperature for 30 minutes to allow flavors to blend. Makes 2/3 cup (150 mL).

Mango Salsa

Tropical fruit in the Mexican mode — accents of lime, coriander and jalapeño — adds fresh zing to grilled fish, chicken and turkey. Canadianize the fruit, if desired, with a peach, juicy pear or tomato instead of the mango.

1/2 cup	diced peeled mango	125 mL
1/2 tsp	minced jalapeño pepper	2 mL
Half	sweet red pepper, diced	Half
Half	small onion, finely chopped	Half
1 tbsp	chopped fresh coriander or parsley	15 mL
1 tbsp	lime juice	15 mL
2 tsp	vegetable oil	10 mL
1	small clove garlic, minced	1
Pinch	each salt and pepper	Pinch

● In nonaluminum bowl, combine mango, jalapeño pepper, red pepper, onion, coriander, lime juice, oil, garlic, salt and pepper.

● Cover and let stand for 1 hour at room temperature or up to 24 hours in refrigerator. Bring to room temperature before serving. Makes 1 cup (250 mL).

Oriental Peanut Sauce

Keep this gingery peanut sauce handy in the refrigerator, ready to spoon over burgers, chicken or pork chops just before giving them one last turn on the grill.

1/4 cup	vegetable oil	50 mL
3 tbsp	rice wine vinegar	45 mL
2 tbsp	soy sauce	25 mL
2 tbsp	water	25 mL
4 tsp	smooth peanut butter	20 mL
1 tbsp	granulated sugar	15 mL
1 tbsp	hoisin sauce	15 mL
2 tsp	sesame oil	10 mL
1 tsp	sweet mustard	5 mL
1/2 tsp	grated gingerroot	2 mL
1/2 tsp	Worcestershire sauce	2 mL
1/4 tsp	hot pepper sauce	1 mL
1	clove garlic, minced	1

● In small saucepan or microwaveable measure, whisk together oil, vinegar, soy sauce, water, peanut butter, sugar, hoisin sauce, sesame oil, mustard, ginger, Worcestershire sauce, hot pepper sauce and garlic.

● Bring to boil; boil for 30 seconds. *(Sauce can be covered and refrigerated for up to 5 days.)* Makes about 3/4 cup (175 mL).

TIP: To give oven-baked chicken that summer-barbecue flavor, brush this sauce generously over chicken parts set, skin side down, on rack in roasting pan. Bake in 375°F (190°C) oven, turning once and brushing with more sauce, for 45 minutes. Crisp chicken under the broiler, if desired.

Light Mayonnaise Sauce

1/2 cup	light mayonnaise	125 mL
1/2 cup	light sour cream	125 mL
3 tbsp	finely chopped dill pickle	50 mL
1 tbsp	grainy mustard	15 mL
1 tbsp	chopped fresh parsley	15 mL
Pinch	each salt and pepper	Pinch

● In bowl, stir together mayonnaise, sour cream, pickle, mustard, parsley, salt and pepper. *(Sauce can be covered and refrigerated for up to 8 hours.)* Makes 1 cup (250 mL).

Enjoy this zesty topping on fish or chicken or lavished onto a burger.

Light Pesto Sauce

2 cups	packed fresh basil leaves	500 mL
2 tbsp	pine nuts	25 mL
2 tbsp	freshly grated Parmesan cheese	25 mL
1/4 tsp	salt	1 mL
1/4 cup	olive oil	50 mL
1	clove garlic, minced	1

● In food processor or blender, finely chop basil, pine nuts, Parmesan cheese and salt. Add oil; purée until smooth. Stir in garlic. *(Sauce can be covered and refrigerated for up to 1 week.)* Makes 3/4 cup (175 mL).

A handy sauce to stir into salad dressing, pesto also makes a full-flavored instant marinade or sauce for grilled chicken and fish.

Hot Honey Mustard

1/4 cup	cider vinegar	50 mL
1/4 cup	liquid honey	50 mL
2 tbsp	packed brown sugar	25 mL
1 tsp	vegetable oil	5 mL
1/4 cup	dry mustard	50 mL
1 tsp	all-purpose flour	5 mL
1/4 tsp	salt	1 mL

● In saucepan, stir together vinegar, honey, brown sugar and oil; cook, stirring, over medium-low heat for 2 minutes.

● Remove from heat; whisk in mustard and flour. Cook, whisking, over medium-high heat for 2 to 3 minutes or until boiling and thickened slightly.

● Reduce heat to medium-low and cook, whisking, for 2 minutes. Stir in salt. Pour into jar; let cool. Seal with tight-fitting lid and refrigerate for 24 hours before serving. *(Mustard can be refrigerated for up to 1 month.)* Makes about 1/2 cup (125 mL).

Liven up a summerful of grilling with your own easy-to-make mustard. Stir a spoonful into potato salad or coleslaw, too.

Zucchini Pepper Relish ▼

A tangy-sweet relish made with summer-harvest vegetables is the perfect topper for burgers and hot dogs. Make a year's supply at one time.

3 lb	zucchini, finely chopped (about 9)	1.5 kg	1/2 tsp	coarsely ground pepper	2 mL
3	onions, finely chopped	3	1/2 tsp	turmeric	2 mL
2	sweet red peppers, seeded and finely chopped	2	1 tbsp	water	15 mL
			2 tsp	cornstarch	10 mL
1/4 cup	pickling salt	50 mL
2-1/2 cups	granulated sugar	625 mL
1-1/2 cups	white vinegar	375 mL
1-1/2 tsp	dry mustard	7 mL
1 tsp	celery seeds	5 mL

● In large bowl, combine zucchini, onions and red peppers; sprinkle with salt and stir to blend. Let stand for 1 hour, stirring occasionally. Drain in large sieve. Rinse thoroughly under cold running water; drain again, pressing out excess moisture.

● In large heavy saucepan, combine sugar, vinegar, mustard, celery seeds, pepper and turmeric; bring to boil. Add drained vegetables and return to boil, stirring frequently.

● Reduce heat and simmer, uncovered and stirring occasionally, for 15 minutes or until vegetables are tender and liquid has thickened.

● Combine water with cornstarch; stir into relish. Cook, stirring, for 5 minutes or until liquid clears and thickens.

● Pour into hot sterilized canning jars, leaving 1/2-inch (1 cm) headspace. Seal with prepared lids and screw on bands. Process in boiling water bath for 10 minutes (see Preserving Basics, next page). Makes 8 cups (2 L).

Ranch-Country Barbecue Sauce

4 cups	ketchup	1 L
1 cup	chili sauce	250 mL
1/4 cup	packed brown sugar	50 mL
1/4 cup	each vegetable oil, water, vinegar and lemon juice	50 mL
2 tbsp	hickory liquid smoke	25 mL
1	lemon, very thinly sliced	1
1	large onion, very thinly sliced	1
1 tsp	each salt, dry mustard and paprika	5 mL

● In large saucepan, combine ketchup, chili sauce, brown sugar, oil, water, vinegar, lemon juice, liquid smoke, lemon, onion, salt, mustard and paprika.

● Bring to boil, stirring frequently to prevent scorching. Partially cover and boil for 4 minutes. *(Sauce can be covered and refrigerated for up to 2 weeks.)* Makes about 6 cups (1.5 L).

*F*rom the foothills of the Rockies comes Lucille Glaister's big-batch barbecue sauce. Brush it over burgers and steaks as they finish their time on the grill — or try it slathered over a roast, ranch-country style.

Smoky Maple Barbecue Sauce

3 tbsp	vegetable oil	50 mL
1	large onion, minced	1
2	large cloves garlic, minced	2
1 tbsp	dry mustard	15 mL
1 tbsp	packed brown sugar	15 mL
1 tbsp	Worcestershire sauce	15 mL
2 tsp	chili powder	10 mL
1 tsp	each celery seeds, dried tarragon and cinnamon	5 mL
3/4 cup	chili sauce	175 mL
1/2 cup	pure maple syrup	125 mL
1/3 cup	orange juice	75 mL
1/4 cup	cider vinegar	50 mL
1/2 tsp	liquid smoke	2 mL
1/4 tsp	salt	1 mL

● In saucepan, heat oil over medium heat; cook onion and garlic for 2 to 3 minutes or until softened.

● Stir in mustard, sugar, Worcestershire sauce, chili powder, celery seeds, tarragon and cinnamon. Add chili sauce, maple syrup, orange juice, vinegar, liquid smoke and salt.

● Simmer, uncovered and stirring often, for 25 minutes or until thickened and glossy. *(Sauce can be covered and refrigerated for up to 1 week.)* Makes 2 cups (500 mL).

*G*lossy all-purpose basting sauce gives a lustrous coating and a tangy-sweet flavor to burgers, ribs, chicken and steaks. Mop it on during the last 15 minutes of grilling time. It's also delicious as a dipping sauce for wings.

PRESERVING BASICS

1 Heat clean canning jars in 225°F (110°C) oven for 15 minutes; leave in oven until needed. Always use new disc part of lid; boil for 5 minutes just before filling jars.

2 Fill boiling water bath canner about two-thirds full of water; bring to gentle boil.

3 Fill jars, leaving 1/2-inch (1 cm) headspace for pickles, relishes and chutneys.

4 Center prepared disc on jar and apply screw band until fingertip tight.

5 Add filled jars to canner; pour in enough boiling water to cover by 2 inches (5 cm). Process for time indicated. Let cool on rack.

6 To check for proper seal, lid should curve down slightly in the center. If lid is flat or bulging, the jar is not sealed and should be

transferred to refrigerator to use within 3 days for fruits and tomatoes, 3 weeks for relishes and salsas.

7 Store jars in cool, dark, dry place. Once jars are opened, store in refrigerator.

Garden Grills

Whether you steam them in packets, skewer them whole or slice them right onto the barbecue, grill-roasted vegetables just taste better! They're fast and no-fuss, too.

Dilly Potato Packets

Pop these packets of potatoes onto the grill 20 to 30 minutes before you plan to serve.

4	scrubbed potatoes	4
1	small onion, diced	1
2 tbsp	chopped fresh dill	25 mL
	Salt and pepper	
1 tbsp	butter	15 mL

● Cut two 12-inch (30 cm) squares of heavy-duty foil; grease shiny side. Cut potatoes into 1/2-inch (1 cm) cubes; divide between squares. Sprinkle with onion, dill, and salt and pepper to taste; dot with butter.

● Loosely wrap foil over vegetables, sealing tightly. Place on grill over medium-high heat; cook, turning once, for 20 to 30 minutes or until tender. Makes 4 servings.

Scalloped Potatoes on the Barbecue ▶

A traditional potato dish takes to the grill. Rosemary is the herb of choice, but dill or parsley are honorable substitutes. Note — this is one place where fresh herbs really count.

1-1/2 lb	scrubbed baking potatoes	750 g
1	large red or cooking onion	1
2 tbsp	butter	25 mL
	Salt and pepper	
1 tbsp	chopped fresh rosemary	15 mL
1/2 cup	creamed cottage cheese	125 mL
1/2 cup	shredded Cheddar cheese	125 mL
1/2 cup	whipping cream	125 mL

● Cut potatoes into 1/2-inch (1 cm) thick slices. Slice onion thinly. Cut butter into small bits.

● On 24-inch (60 cm) square of greased heavy-duty foil, arrange half of the potato slices in single layer. Top with half of the onion slices. Dot with half of the butter. Sprinkle with salt and pepper to taste, then with some of the rosemary.

● Evenly spread cottage cheese over potatoes; sprinkle with Cheddar cheese. Layer with remaining onion; sprinkle with salt and pepper to taste and remaining rosemary. Top with remaining potatoes; dot with remaining butter.

● Fold foil over and seal 2 of the edges together with double fold. Tilting open end up slightly, pour in cream; seal foil tightly.

● Place on grill over medium heat; cover and cook for 20 minutes. Carefully turn package over; cook for 10 to 20 minutes longer or until potatoes are tender. Makes 4 servings.

POTATOES ON THE GRILL

Potatoes are a real treat hot off the grill. They round out any summertime meal wonderfully.

BAKING POTATOES

● Prick white baking or sweet potatoes, brush with oil, if desired, and wrap in foil. Cook in a covered barbecue over medium heat, turning often, for about 50 minutes.

ONION FAN POTATOES

● Slice potatoes at 1/4-inch (5 mm) intervals almost to the bottom. Insert slices of red or cooking onion into spaces. Place each potato on foil square and drizzle slices with melted butter or oil plus herbs, if desired. Season with salt and pepper, seal tightly and cook, turning once, for about 1 hour.

THICK POTATO SLICES

● Brush thick unpeeled potato or sweet potato slices with mixture of equal parts vegetable oil and vinegar. Cook on greased grill for about 5 minutes on each side or until tender. Sprinkle with salt, pepper and chopped chives.

POTATOES ON SKEWERS

● Use about 1 lb (500 g) small new potatoes for 4 people; scrub well but do not peel. Microwave, boil or steam before threading onto skewers.

To microwave: Pierce potatoes; place in shallow dish with 1/4 cup (50 mL) water. Cover and microwave at High, stirring once, for 7 to 10 minutes or until just tender. Let stand for 3 minutes; drain well.

To boil: In saucepan, cover potatoes with cold water. Bring to boil; boil for 10 to 15 minutes or until almost tender.

To steam: Place in top of double boiler set over boiling water; steam for 10 to 15 minutes or until almost tender.

● Place skewers on greased grill over medium-high heat; cook, brushing often with olive oil or with seasoned butter (see below), for 6 to 10 minutes or until heated through and skins are crisp.

SEASONED BUTTERS

● To add extra flavor to potato skewers on the grill, brush often with one of these easy butters. Each makes enough for 1 lb (500 g) cooked new potatoes.

Sage Butter: In bowl, stir together 3 tbsp (50 mL) melted butter, 2 tbsp (25 mL) chopped fresh sage and 1/4 tsp (1 mL) each salt and pepper.

Chive Butter: In bowl, stir together 3 tbsp (50 mL) melted butter, 2 tbsp (25 mL) each chopped chives and green onions, 1 tbsp (15 mL) each grated lemon rind and juice, 1/2 tsp (2 mL) salt and 1/4 tsp (1 mL) pepper.

Garlic Butter: In bowl, stir together 3 tbsp (50 mL) melted butter, 1 tbsp (15 mL) chopped fresh parsley, 4 minced cloves garlic, 2 minced green onions and 1/4 tsp (1 mL) each salt and pepper.

Sesame Coriander Butter: In bowl, stir together 1 tbsp (15 mL) chopped fresh coriander, 1 tbsp (15 mL) olive oil, 1 tsp (5 mL) soy sauce, 1/2 tsp (2 mL) sesame oil and 2 minced cloves garlic.

A Package of Mushrooms and Onions

3/4 lb	mushrooms, sliced	375 g
2	large onions, thinly sliced	2
1	clove garlic, minced	1
3 tbsp	olive oil	50 mL
1 tbsp	chopped fresh thyme	15 mL
1/2 tsp	salt	2 mL
1/4 tsp	pepper	1 mL

● In bowl, toss together mushrooms, onions, garlic, oil, thyme, salt and pepper. Divide between two large pieces of heavy-duty foil. Loosely wrap foil over vegetables, sealing tightly.

● Place on grill over medium heat; cook for about 20 minutes or until tender. Makes 4 servings.

A superb side dish, these herbed onions also make a juicy topping for grilled steak or baked potatoes. (In photo, with Grilled Marinated Steak, p. 9.)

Thyme for Carrots

1 lb	small carrots (about 12)	500 g
1/2 cup	chopped red onion	125 mL
4 tsp	butter	20 mL
2 tsp	chopped fresh thyme	10 mL
	Salt and pepper	

● Divide carrots between two pieces of heavy-duty foil large enough to fold into packets.

● Sprinkle evenly with onion, butter and thyme; season with salt and pepper to taste. Loosely wrap foil over carrots, sealing tightly.

● Place on grill over medium-high heat; cook, turning once, for 20 to 25 minutes or until tender-crisp. Makes 4 servings.

Small summer carrots suit package cooking. Vary the herbs, if you like — mint, marjoram and parsley all play up the natural sweetness of carrots.

Leeks on the Grill

8	small leeks (white and light green parts)	8
Pinch	each salt and pepper	Pinch
1 tbsp	butter	15 mL
1 tsp	olive oil	5 mL
1 tsp	balsamic vinegar	5 mL

● Trim leeks; cut in half lengthwise. Rinse under running water, spreading leaves to remove grit; pat dry.

● Place leeks in center of large piece of heavy-duty foil. Season with salt and pepper; dot with butter. Loosely wrap foil over leeks, sealing tightly.

● Place on grill over medium-high heat; cook, turning once, for 20 to 30 minutes or until tender. Arrange on serving plate.

● Combine oil and vinegar; drizzle over leeks. Makes 4 servings.

Look for small leeks with the highest proportion of white to green — they'll grill up to a sweet and tender taste. (In photo, with Grilled Mustard Dill Fish, p. 51.)

Gremolada Tomatoes ▶

Lemon rind, parsley and garlic add the gremolada touch to summer-fresh tomatoes (photo, next page) or to a fish fillet or chicken breast as it finishes on the grill.

2	cloves garlic, minced	2
2 tbsp	chopped fresh parsley	25 mL
1 tsp	grated lemon rind	5 mL
1 tbsp	lemon juice	15 mL
1/4 tsp	salt	1 mL
Pinch	pepper	Pinch
4	tomatoes	4

● Whisk together garlic, parsley, lemon rind and juice, salt and pepper.

● Cut tomatoes in half. Place, cut side up, on greased grill over medium heat; top evenly with parsley mixture. Cook for 15 to 20 minutes or until softened and tender throughout. Makes 4 servings.

Roasted Garlic ▶

Whole fresh heads of fat garlic cloves, slowly roasted on the grill, caramelize and mellow into a great appetizer (see photo, next page). Press out each clove and spread on grilled Italian bread.

4	whole heads garlic	4
2 tbsp	olive oil	25 mL
4	sprigs fresh thyme or rosemary	4

● Rub off papery outer layers of garlic heads. Cut off about 1/4 inch (5 mm) from tips. Arrange in double thickness of heavy-duty foil; drizzle with oil and top with thyme.

● Loosely wrap foil over garlic, sealing tightly. Cook on grill over low heat for about 1 hour or until soft and tender. To serve, squeeze out pulp. Makes 4 to 6 servings.

TIP: If you like, smash the soft cloves and whisk into mayo to spread over burger buns, or stir mashed clove into a vinaigrette to toss with new potatoes or greens.

VEGETABLES ON THE GRILL

Vegetables such as eggplant, zucchini, summer squash, onions and mushrooms are best grilled as they are without prior cooking. For small pieces of vegetables, use greased mesh grill set on barbecue.

● **Eggplant:** Cut into 1/4- to 1/2-inch (5 mm to 1 cm) thick slices; brush lightly with oil. Place on greased grill; cook, turning once, for 10 minutes.

● **Onions:** Cut into 1/2-inch (1 cm) thick slices. Crisscross 2 toothpicks through thickness of each slice to form X; brush with oil. Place on grill; cook, turning several times, for about 10 minutes.

● **Zucchini and Summer Squash:** Cut crosswise on diagonal or lengthwise into 1/2-inch (1 cm) thick slices; brush lightly with oil. Place on greased grill; cook, turning once, for 8 to 10 minutes.

● **Mushrooms:** Keep whole; trim ends of stems. Brush lightly with oil. Place on greased grill, cap side down; cook for 12 to 15 minutes.

In photo: Beer-Marinated Barbecued Pork Chop (p. 20), Gremolada Tomato and Roasted Garlic (above), Summer Grilled Chicken (p. 46), cherry tomatoes and small onions on skewer, grilled carrot, green onion, halved sweet yellow and green pepper, zucchini and shiitake mushrooms.

Zucchinibobs

Tangy sweet balsamic vinegar adds punch to grilled zucchini. (In photo, with Herb and Buttermilk Barbecued Chicken, p. 38.)

2	each green and gold zucchini	2
2 tbsp	balsamic or red wine vinegar	25 mL
1	clove garlic, minced	1
2 tsp	Dijon mustard	10 mL
1/2 tsp	dried oregano	2 mL
1/4 tsp	each dried thyme, salt and pepper	1 mL
3 tbsp	olive oil	50 mL

● Cut green and gold zucchini in half lengthwise; cut into chunks. Set aside.

● In large bowl, whisk together vinegar, garlic, mustard, oregano, thyme, salt and pepper; gradually whisk in oil. Add zucchini, tossing to coat; let stand at room temperature for up to 1 hour.

● Reserving marinade, thread zucchini colors alternately onto each of 4 long skewers. Place on greased grill over medium-high heat; cook, turning often and brushing with marinade, for about 8 minutes or until tender-crisp. Makes 4 servings.

Grilled Vegetable Salad

With its smoky grilled flavors and tangy vinaigrette, this make-ahead salad is sure to be a hit.

1	large eggplant	1
	Salt	
1	each sweet red and yellow pepper	1
2	zucchini	2
1	red onion	1
12	mushrooms	12
	Olive oil	
1	tomato, chopped	1
1/3 cup	slivered black olives	75 mL
	DRESSING	
1/4 cup	balsamic or red wine vinegar	50 mL
1 tbsp	Dijon mustard	15 mL
2	cloves garlic, minced	2
1/2 tsp	each salt and pepper	2 mL
1/3 cup	chopped fresh basil	75 mL
1/2 cup	olive oil	125 mL

● Cut eggplant into 1-inch (2.5 cm) thick slices; layer in colander, sprinkling each layer lightly with salt. Let drain for 30 minutes.

● Meanwhile, place red and yellow peppers on greased grill over medium-high heat; cook, turning often, for about 10 minutes or until lightly roasted. Let cool slightly. Peel, seed and cut into 1-inch (2.5 cm) squares. Place in large bowl.

● Cut zucchini and onion into 1/2-inch (1 cm) thick slices. Trim ends of mushroom stems. Rinse eggplant under cold water; pat dry.

● Lightly brush vegetables and mushrooms with oil. Place mushrooms and onion on grill; cook, turning occasionally, for 8 to 10 minutes. Place zucchini and eggplant on grill; cook, turning once, for 10 minutes or until well-marked but still slightly firm. Halve zucchini, quarter onion and cube eggplant slices; add to sweet peppers along with mushrooms.

● DRESSING: In bowl, whisk together vinegar, mustard, garlic, salt and pepper; whisk in basil, then oil, in steady stream. Pour over vegetables, tossing gently to coat.

● Refrigerate salad for at least 4 hours or up to 8 hours. Bring to room temperature before serving. Garnish with tomato and olives. Makes 6 servings.

WHAT A GREAT IDEA!

Use your grill to warm a light vinaigrette, then toss with mixed greens.
● In saucepan on edge of grill, heat 1/2 cup (125 mL) vegetable oil, 3 tbsp (50 mL) white wine vinegar and 1 or 2 tbsp (15 or 25 mL) of your favorite herb — coriander, basil, dill, tarragon or parsley.

Embered Onions

12	baby onions (unpeeled)	12
1/4 cup	vegetable oil	50 mL
1/4 cup	rice vinegar	50 mL
1 tbsp *	molasses	15 mL
2 tsp	chopped fresh thyme, sage or rosemary	10 mL
1/2 tsp	salt	2 mL
	Fresh thyme, sage or rosemary sprigs	

● Slice root end off onions; place in bowl. Pour in enough boiling water to cover; let stand for 10 minutes. Drain and peel; arrange in single layer in shallow glass dish.

● Combine oil, vinegar, molasses, thyme and salt; pour over onions, rolling to coat. Cover and marinate in refrigerator for at least 12 hours or up to 48 hours. Let stand at room temperature for 30 minutes.

● Reserving marinade, thread onions onto 4 short metal skewers, sandwiching thyme sprigs between onions. Place on greased grill over medium heat; cook, turning and basting often with marinade, for about 1 hour or until tender and deep golden brown. Makes 4 servings.

*S*low-cook small mature onions until their skin crisps and the insides soften into melt-in-your-mouth sweetness.

MICRO-GRILLED VEGETABLES

Firm vegetables are the stars of the micro-grill two-step. Here are a few ways to enjoy them with all the grill flavors — fast!

CORN: Arrange 4 to 6 husked corn cobs in a circle with thick ends to outside; microwave, covered, at High for 2 to 3 minutes per cob or just until tender. Let stand for 5 minutes. Brush with oil and cook on grill, turning, until hot and lightly grill-marked.

SQUASH: Prick pepper (acorn) squash several times; microwave at High for 8 to 10 minutes or until barely fork-tender. Quarter and seed; cook on grill, brushing with herb-flavored oil or with maple syrup, until hot and burnished brown.

CARROTS AND SMALL ONIONS: In large measure, microwave at High with 2 tbsp (25 mL) water until just tender; thread onto skewers. Brush with oil and sprinkle with herbs; cook on grill until hot and grill-marked.

Hot and New

Quesadillas, roasted pepper sandwiches and nineties-style pizzas and tortillas take to the grill for some of the hottest new tastes in town.

Grilled Quesadillas ▶

*T*ortilla foldovers filled with Mexican-style beans, salsa and cheese are one of the trendiest quick-eats around. Just add a salad, and you have an effortless dinner for four.

4	10-inch (25 cm) flour tortillas	4
1	can (19 oz/540 mL) kidney beans, rinsed and drained	1
1 cup	Peppy Salsa (recipe, p. 68)	250 mL
4	green onions, chopped	4
1/4 cup	chopped green olives	50 mL
2 tbsp	chopped fresh coriander or parsley	25 mL
1-1/3 cups	shredded extra-old Cheddar cheese	325 mL

● Arrange tortillas on work surface. In bowl and using potato masher, mash beans along with 1/2 cup (125 mL) of the salsa. Divide among tortillas, spreading evenly and leaving 1/2-inch (1 cm) border.

● Sprinkle bean mixture with onions, then olives; sprinkle with coriander, then cheese. Fold tortillas over and press gently to seal.

● Place on greased grill over medium-high heat; cook, turning halfway through, for 8 to 10 minutes or until browned and crisped. Garnish with remaining salsa. Makes 4 servings.

Roasted Red Pepper and Eggplant Sandwich

*I*f you have never tasted a grilled eggplant sandwich, you're in for a treat! While these sandwiches are vegetarian, their great grill-roasted flavor makes them popular with everybody. Be sure to use Russian-style mustard.

1	small eggplant	1
	Salt	
2	sweet red peppers	2
1 tbsp	olive oil	15 mL
8	slices pumpernickel bread	8
2 tbsp	sweet prepared mustard	25 mL
4	lettuce leaves	4
3 oz	fontina cheese	75 g

● Cut eggplant into 1/4-inch (5 mm) thick slices; place in colander and sprinkle with salt. Let stand for 30 minutes.

● Meanwhile, place peppers on greased grill over medium-high heat; cook, turning often, for 20 to 25 minutes or until charred. Let cool slightly; peel, seed and cut into quarters. Set aside.

● Rinse eggplant under cold water; pat dry. Brush with oil. Place on grill; cook, turning occasionally, for about 10 minutes or until tender but not charred. Set aside.

● Place bread on grill; cook, turning once, for 3 to 4 minutes or until toasted. Spread one side of each slice with mustard.

● Layer lettuce, eggplant, red pepper and cheese on half of the slices. Top with remaining slices. Makes 4 servings.

Yellow Pepper and Tomato Bruschetta

"Brushetta or brusketta?" No matter how you pronounce it, this popular Italian appetizer (photo, p. 44) is perfect on its own or partnered with grilled meat or fish.

3	cloves garlic, minced	3
2	tomatoes, seeded and diced	2
1	sweet yellow or green pepper, diced	1
1/4 cup	chopped fresh basil	50 mL
	Salt and pepper	
	French baguette or crusty Italian bread	
1/4 cup	olive oil	50 mL

● In bowl, combine two-thirds of the garlic, the tomatoes, yellow pepper, basil, and salt and pepper to taste.

● Slice bread diagonally into 3/4-inch (2 cm) thick slices. Combine remaining garlic with oil; brush over one side of each slice. Place, garlic side down, on greased grill over medium heat; cook for 1 to 2 minutes or until golden.

● Spoon tomato mixture onto grilled side of bread; cook for 8 to 10 minutes or until heated through. Makes about 6 servings.

Cheesy Grilled Vegetable Pie

Grilling the vegetables for this deep-dish pie adds a wonderful smoky-rich flavor that balances beautifully with the creamy cheese filling. Serve warm from the oven or at room temperature.

1	eggplant	1
3/4 tsp	salt	4 mL
2	sweet red peppers	2
2	zucchini	2
1 tbsp	olive oil	15 mL
	Pastry for 10-inch (25 cm) double-crust pie	
1 tbsp	Dijon mustard	15 mL
1 cup	shredded mozzarella or Fontina cheese	250 mL
8 oz	ricotta cheese	250 g
2	eggs	2
1/4 cup	chopped fresh basil (or 1-1/2 tsp/7 mL dried)	50 mL
1/4 tsp	(approx) dried marjoram	1 mL
Pinch	pepper	Pinch
3/4 cup	freshly grated Parmesan cheese	175 mL
1	egg white, beaten	1

● Cut eggplant lengthwise into 1/4-inch (5 mm) thick slices. Place in colander and sprinkle with 1/2 tsp (2 mL) of the salt. Let stand for 30 minutes; rinse and pat dry.

● Meanwhile, place red peppers on greased grill over high heat; cook, turning often, for about 20 minutes or until charred. Let cool slightly; peel and seed. Set aside.

● Slice zucchini lengthwise into 1/4-inch (5 mm) thick slices; place on grill and cook for 5 minutes or until tender and lightly browned.

● Lightly brush eggplant with oil; place on grill and cook for 5 minutes on each side or until tender. Chop red peppers, zucchini and eggplant into bite-size pieces; let cool completely.

● On lightly floured surface, roll out half of the pastry and fit into 10-inch (25 cm) pie plate; brush with mustard. Sprinkle with 1/2 cup (125 mL) of the mozzarella and half of the chopped vegetables.

● Combine ricotta, eggs, basil, remaining salt, 1/4 tsp (1 mL) marjoram, pepper, remaining mozzarella and 1/2 cup (125 mL) of the Parmesan cheese. Spread evenly over vegetables. Top with remaining vegetables; sprinkle with remaining Parmesan.

● Moisten pastry rim with water. Roll out remaining pastry and place over filling; seal, trim and flute edges. Brush with egg white; sprinkle with more marjoram. Cut three slashes in top crust.

● Bake in 425°F (220°C) oven for 40 minutes or until golden. Makes 8 servings.

Focaccia Eggplant Sandwich

1	large eggplant	1
	Vegetable oil	
1	long focaccia bread	1
2	tomatoes, cored and thinly sliced	2
1 cup	shredded Asiago cheese	250 mL
	OLIVE PASTE	
1/4 cup	pitted black olives	50 mL
2 tbsp	light mayonnaise	25 mL
1 tbsp	olive oil	15 mL
1	clove garlic, minced	1

● OLIVE PASTE: In blender, purée olives, mayonnaise and oil until smooth; stir in garlic. Set aside.

● Cut eggplant into 1/4-inch (5 mm) thick slices. Brush lightly with oil. Place on greased grill over medium-high heat; cook, turning occasionally, for about 10 minutes or until tender but not charred. Set aside.

● Cut focaccia in half lengthwise; spread olive paste over one half. Layer with half of the eggplant, all of the tomatoes, the remaining eggplant, then the cheese. Place remaining half of focaccia over top.

● Wrap tightly with foil; refrigerate for at least 2 hours or up to 6 hours. Let stand at room temperature for 30 minutes.

● Place wrapped sandwich on grill over medium-high heat; cook for 15 to 20 minutes or until warmed through and cheese has melted. Remove foil. Serve warm. Makes 4 servings.

Eggplant, black olives and Asiago cheese — what a wonderful marriage of flavors! The inspiration for this satisfying sandwich comes from the Mildred Pierce restaurant in Toronto.

QUICK TORTILLA PIZZAS

For summertime pizzas in a hurry, top a flour tortilla with your choice of Basil and Tomato, Greek or Mexicano ingredients (see below). Place on greased grill over medium heat and cook for 5 to 7 minutes or until tortilla is crisp and cheese has melted. Makes 2 servings.

BASIL AND TOMATO

1	tomato, seeded and diced	1
1	clove garlic, minced	1
1 tbsp	chopped fresh basil	15 mL
	Salt and pepper	
1/2 cup	shredded mozzarella cheese	125 mL
1	10-inch (25 cm) flour tortilla	1
1 tbsp	freshly grated Parmesan cheese	15 mL

● In bowl, combine tomato, garlic and basil; season with salt and pepper to taste. Sprinkle half of the mozzarella over tortilla; top with tomato mixture. Sprinkle with Parmesan and remaining mozzarella cheese.

THE GREEK CONNECTION

1	10-inch (25 cm) flour tortilla	1
1/3 cup	crumbled feta cheese	75 mL
1/3 cup	chopped sweet green pepper	75 mL
2 tbsp	slivered black olives	25 mL
1 tbsp	chopped fresh oregano	15 mL

● Sprinkle tortilla with feta cheese, green pepper, olives and oregano.

MEXICANO

1	tomato, seeded and diced	1
1	clove garlic, minced	1
Half	jalapeño pepper, finely chopped	Half
1 tbsp	chopped fresh coriander	15 mL
	Salt and pepper	
1/2 cup	shredded Monterey Jack cheese	125 mL
1	10-inch (25 cm) flour tortilla	1

● In bowl, combine tomato, garlic, jalapeño pepper and coriander; season with salt and pepper to taste. Sprinkle half of the cheese over tortilla; top with tomato mixture. Sprinkle with remaining cheese.

Grilled Summer Pizza

Pizza cooked on the barbecue? Why not, especially when a barbecue with cover becomes an instant alfresco range. This recipe is complete with toppings and a pizza base. For pizza in a hurry, simply buy prebaked pizza rounds or refrigerated or frozen pizza dough.

	Cornmeal	
1	bunch broccoli	1
2 cups	shredded fontina cheese	500 mL
1 cup	shredded mozzarella cheese	250 mL
2	cloves garlic, minced	2
1	small red onion, sliced	1
3 cups	sliced mushrooms (about 1/2 lb/250 g)	750 mL
8	cherry tomatoes, cut into thirds	8
2 oz	prosciutto or ham, cut into strips	60 g
1/4 cup	freshly grated Parmesan cheese	50 mL
1/4 cup	shredded fresh basil	50 mL
	CRUST	
2-1/2 cups	all-purpose flour	625 mL
1	pkg quick-rising (instant) dry yeast	1
1 tsp	salt	5 mL
1/2 tsp	granulated sugar	2 mL
1 tbsp	olive oil	15 mL

● CRUST: In large bowl, combine 1-3/4 cups (425 mL) of the flour, yeast, salt and sugar. With wooden spoon, stir in 1 cup (250 mL) very hot water (120°F-130°F/50°C-55°C) and oil. Beat in enough of the remaining flour to make firm but soft dough. Turn out onto lightly floured surface; knead for 10 minutes or until smooth and elastic. Cover and let stand for 10 minutes.

● Dust two 12-inch (30 cm) round pizza pans with cornmeal. On lightly floured surface, roll out half of the dough into 13-inch (33 cm) circle for each pizza; place on pan, folding excess dough underneath.

● Cut broccoli into bite-size pieces. In pot of boiling water, cook for 3 minutes. Drain and refresh under cold water; drain again.

● Combine Fontina and mozzarella cheeses; sprinkle 1/2 cup (125 mL) over each crust. Top each evenly with broccoli, garlic, onion, mushrooms, tomatoes and prosciutto. Sprinkle with remaining cheese mixture and Parmesan.

● Place on grill over medium-high heat; cover and cook, rotating pans once, for about 12 minutes or until crust is crisp and cheese has melted. Sprinkle with basil. Makes 6 servings.

PIZZA ON THE GRILL
A perforated pizza pan is ideal on the grill since it allows the heat to crisp the crust while the toppings melt and cook.

Alfresco Pepperoni Pizza

Thanks to prebaked pizza crusts, a Friday-night favorite comes to the barbecue. Replace the pepperoni with prosciutto, smoked turkey or chorizo, if you like.

1	10-inch (25 cm) prebaked pizza crust	1
4 tsp	olive oil	20 mL
1-3/4 cups	shredded mozzarella cheese	425 mL
1	sweet green or yellow pepper, cut into rings	1
4 oz	pepperoni, sliced	125 g
Pinch	each salt and pepper	Pinch

● Place pizza crust on perforated pizza pan. Brush with oil; sprinkle with half of the cheese. Arrange green pepper, then pepperoni, in single layers over top. Sprinkle with salt, pepper and remaining cheese.

● Place on grill over medium-high heat; cover and cook, rotating pan once, for about 12 minutes or until crust is crisp and cheese has melted. Makes 2 to 4 servings.

Four-Cheese Pizza

1	10-inch (25 cm) prebaked pizza crust	1
4 tsp	olive oil	20 mL
1/2 cup	shredded mozzarella cheese	125 mL
1/2 cup	shredded fontina cheese	125 mL
1/2 cup	shredded provolone cheese	125 mL
1	large tomato, cored and sliced	1
2 tbsp	freshly grated Parmesan cheese	25 mL
2 tbsp	chopped fresh basil	25 mL

● Place pizza crust on perforated pizza pan; brush with oil. Combine mozzarella, fontina and provolone cheeses; sprinkle half over crust.

● Arrange tomato in single layer over top, overlapping slightly if necessary. Sprinkle with remaining cheese mixture; sprinkle with Parmesan.

● Place on grill over medium-high heat; cover and cook, rotating pan once, for about 12 minutes or until crust is crisp and cheese has melted. Sprinkle with basil. Makes 2 to 4 servings.

Once you've tasted this rich and flavorful pizza, "double cheese" will never be enough again!

Summer Bounty Pizza

1	10-inch (25 cm) prebaked pizza crust	1
4 tsp	olive oil	20 mL
1-1/4 cups	shredded mozzarella cheese	300 mL
1	small zucchini, thinly sliced	1
2	tomatoes, thinly sliced	2
6	pitted black olives, slivered	6
1	clove garlic, minced	1
1/2 tsp	dried thyme	2 mL
2 oz	goat cheese, crumbled	50 g

● Place pizza crust on perforated pizza pan. Brush with oil; sprinkle with mozzarella. Arrange zucchini, then tomatoes, in single layer on top. Sprinkle with olives, garlic and thyme; top with goat cheese.

● Place on grill over medium-high heat; cover and cook, rotating pan once, for about 12 minutes or until crust is crisp and cheese has melted. Makes 2 to 4 servings.

For a quick and easy summertime pizza, top the crust high with your favorite garden-fresh vegetables.

TIP: To blanch firm vegetables such as broccoli and carrots before adding to pizzas, drop bite-size pieces or slices into large pot of boiling water. Boil for 1 to 3 minutes or until tender-crisp; remove with slotted spoon and immediately chill in cold water. Remove and let drain on paper towels.

DESSERTS ON THE GRILL

Summertime meals are especially relaxing when everything can be done on the barbecue — including dessert! Here are two easy sweet endings.

Fresh Berries with Warm Vinaigrette

● In saucepan, heat 1/4 cup (50 mL) balsamic vinegar and 2 tbsp (25 mL) packed brown sugar on edge of grill. Drizzle vinaigrette over large serving bowl of fresh strawberries.

Fruit Fondue

● Turn off barbecue. In small heavy saucepan, combine 1/2 cup (125 mL) chocolate chips and 2 tbsp (25 mL) whipping cream. Place on grill and close cover; let stand for 5 to 10 minutes or until chocolate is melted.

● Arrange fresh berries, pineapple spears, banana chunks and apple wedges on platter; provide toothpicks for dipping fruit into chocolate sauce.

The Contributors

For your easy reference, we have included an alphabetical listing of recipes by contributor.

Julian Armstrong
Lamb Burgers, 66
Lamb Chops à la Madame
    Benoit, 32
Lamb Kabobs, 30
Lamb Shoulder with Thyme
    and Garlic, 35

Elizabeth Baird
Barbecued Whitefish, 57
Focaccia Eggplant
    Sandwich, 85
Grilled Racks of Lamb with
    Thyme, 35
Oriental Fish Kabobs with
    Green Onions, 50
Oriental Peanut Sauce, 70
Roasted Red Pepper and
    Eggplant Sandwich, 82

Keith Bennett
Real Barbecued Pork, 22

Vicki Burns
Grilled Chicken and Tomato
    Salad, 45
Herb and Buttermilk
    Barbecued Chicken, 39
Lemon Pepper Marinade, 38
Lime Cumin Marinade, 38
Souvlaki, 27
Teriyaki Chicken and
    Vegetable Slaw, 45
Thai Marinade, 38
Zucchinibobs, 80

Cynthia David
Crisp Grilled Squid, 56
Dilly Potato Packets, 74
Grilled Mustard Dill
    Fish, 51

Leeks on the Grill, 77
Mango Salsa, 70
Salade Niçoise, 53
Tarragon Lemon
    Marinade, 50
Teriyaki Marinade, 50
Warm Paella Salad, 53

Margaret Fraser
Barbecued Turkey, 47
Chicken and Veggie
    Packets, 36
Desserts on the Grill, 87
Grilled Steak Salad, 11
Maple-Glazed Thighs, 44
Micro-Grilled Korean
    Ribs, 16

Joanne Good
Easy Alberta Sirloin Slab, 10
Fine Barbecued Rib
    Roast, 12
Ranch-Country Barbecue
    Sauce, 73

Peter Gzowski
Scalloped Potatoes on the
    Barbecue, 74

Rose Murray
Apple Thyme Pork
    Chops, 22
Barbecued Spareribs with
    Apple-Sage Glaze, 19
Beer-Glazed Picnic
    Shoulder, 23
Caesar Burgers, 62
Cod with Lemon-Dill
    Mayo, 50
Hoisin Orange Chicken
    Legs, 41

Honey Mustard Sausages, 28
Mushroom Barbecued Pot
    Roast, 13
Santa Fe Short Ribs, 13
Turkey Burgers with Kiwi
    Salsa, 63

Daphna Rabinovitch
Curried Shrimp for Two, 57
Grilled Summer Pizza, 86
Sticky Red-Hot Ribs, 16

Iris Raven
Hot Honey Mustard, 71

Marg Routledge
Tangy Pork Kabobs, 26

Judy Schultz
Beer-Marinated Barbecued
    Pork Chops, 20
Embered Onions, 81
Fajitas with Peppers and
    Apples, 27
Osaka-Style Marinade, 20
Honey-Mustard
    Marinade, 20
Thai-Style Pork Salad, 27

Edena Sheldon
Barbecued Brisket of Beef
    Sandwich Feast, 15
Devilled Beef Ribs, 14
Greek Beef Burgers, 60
Lime and Mint-Glazed Flank
    Steak, 10
Provençal Beef Brochettes, 6
Smoky Maple Barbecue
    Sauce, 73
T-Bone Steaks with Herb
    Garlic Butter, 8

Kay Spicer
Apple-Stuffed Pork
Burgers, 62
Peking Ribs, 19

Bonnie Stern
Cajun Chicken Livers, 43
Creole Superburger, 58
Garlicky Curry Skewered
Fish, 52
Hoisin Orange Pork
Chops, 20

David Veljacic
Party-Size Barbecued Pork
Roast, 24
Prize-Winning Barbecued
Salmon, 48

Julie Watson
Lime-Grilled Lobster, 54
Mussels with Lemon Garlic
Butter, 54

Canadian Living Test Kitchen
A Package of Mushrooms
and Onions, 77
Alfresco Pepperoni
Pizza, 86
Balsamic Butterflied
Lamb, 35
Balsamic Rosemary
Marinade, 9

Cheesy Grilled Vegetable
Pie, 84
Chicken Burgers
Provençal, 65
Curried Rice and Beef
Salad, 15
Curry Lime Kabobs, 25
Five-Spice Grilled Chicken
Breasts, 39
Four-Cheese Pizza, 87
Garlic Seafood Skewers, 55
Greek Marinade, 9
Gremolada Tomatoes, 78
Grilled Beef and Sweet
Pepper Sandwiches, 14
Grilled Fillet Burgers, 64
Grilled Pickerel Skewers, 52
Grilled Quesadillas, 82
Grilled Salmon Fillets, 48
Grilled Sausage on a
Bun, 28
Grilled Teriyaki Pork
Tenderloin, 24
Grilled Vegetable Salad, 80
Herbed Lamb Chops, 30
Herbed Parmesan Chicken
Burgers, 66
Jerk Chicken on the Grill, 40
Korean Marinade, 9
Lamb Chops with Red
Pepper Pesto, 33
Lemon Rainbow Trout, 54
Lemon Rosemary
Chicken, 44
Light Mayonnaise Sauce, 71

Light Pesto Sauce, 71
Mediterranean Burgers with
Cucumber Pickles, 65
Micro-Grill Moroccan
Chicken, 43
Orange-Glazed Leg of
Lamb, 34
Oriental Black Bean
Spareribs, 17
Peppy Salsa, 68
Pizza Burgers, 61
Potatoes on the Grill, 76
Prosciutto-Wrapped
Chicken Breasts, 36
Quick Tortilla Pizzas, 85
Reuben Burger Melts, 67
Roasted Garlic, 78
Rosemary Mustard Chicken
Breasts, 39
Salsa Burgers, 61
Skewers of Chicken and
Zucchini, 40
Summer Bounty Pizza, 87
Summer Grilled Chicken, 46
Tender Marinated Steak, 8
Thai Barbecued Chicken, 46
Thyme for Carrots, 77
Tofu Burgers in Pita
Pockets, 67
Tomato Rosemary Salsa, 70
Vegetables on the Grill, 78
Yellow Pepper and Tomato
Bruschetta, 84
Your Basic Burger, 60
Zucchini Pepper Relish, 72

Photography Credits
FRED BIRD:
front and back covers,
copyright page, pages 7, 9,
12, 17, 18, 20, 23, 25, 26, 32,
33, 37, 38, 41, 44, 47, 49, 51,
55, 58, 63, 64, 69, 72, 75, 76,
79, 81, 83, 96.

CHRISTOPHER
CAMPBELL:
pages 56, 71.

NEW ZEALAND
LAMB COMPANY:
page 31.

ONTARIO SHEEP
MARKETING AGENCY:
page 34.

BOB WIGINGTON:
page 42.

STANLEY WONG:
page 29.

Special Thanks

Acknowledging the people who have made *Canadian Living's Best Barbecue* is a pleasure. The creativity, meticulous eye and organizing skills of Madison Press project editor Wanda Nowakowska are first in line for appreciation, as are Beverley Renahan, *Canadian Living* senior editor, and Daphna Rabinovitch, manager of *Canadian Living's* Test Kitchen. Others at the magazine are due sincere thanks as well: Test Kitchen staff shown on the front flap, plus Vicki Burns, Janet Cornish and Christine Levac, and senior editor Donna Paris. Our "looks good enough to eat" photography comes largely via the skills of creative director Deborah Fadden, food stylists Jennifer McLagan and Olga Truchan, and photographer Fred Bird, and the clean user-friendly design from Gord Sibley. Dinners across Canada are all the tastier because of the contributions of *Canadian Living's* very accomplished food writers, the finest in the land. Of course, all of our work at *Canadian Living* is under the guidance of editor-in-chief Bonnie Cowan and publisher Kirk Shearer, whose commitment to *The Best* series is wonderful encouragement.

Elizabeth Baird

Index

EDITORIAL DIRECTOR
Hugh Brewster

PROJECT EDITOR
Wanda Nowakowska

EDITORIAL ASSISTANCE
Beverley Renahan

PRODUCTION DIRECTOR
Susan Barrable

PRODUCTION COORDINATOR
Donna Chong

BOOK DESIGN AND LAYOUT
Gordon Sibley Design Inc.

COLOR SEPARATION
Colour Technologies

PRINTING AND BINDING
Friesen Printers

CANADIAN LIVING ADVISORY BOARD
Robert A. Murray, Kirk Shearer, Caren King,
Bonnie Baker Cowan, Elizabeth Baird, Anna Hobbs

CANADIAN LIVING'S™ BEST BARBECUE
was produced by Madison Press Books
under the direction of Albert E. Cummings